*Managing Rental
Properties
for Maximum Profit*

How to Order:

Quantity discounts are available from the publisher, Prima Publishing, P.O. Box 1260BK, Rocklin, CA 95677; telephone: (916) 632-4400. On your letterhead include information concerning the intended use of the books and the number of books you wish to purchase.

Managing Rental Properties for Maximum Profit

Greg Perry

Prima Publishing
P.O. Box 1260BK
Rocklin, CA 95677
(916) 632-4400

Copy editing by Candace Demeduc
Production by Melanie Field, Bookman Productions
Typography by AeroType, Inc.
Interior design by Judith Levinson
Jacket by The Dunlavey Studio

Lotus 1-2-3 is a registered trademark of Lotus Development Corporation.
Microsoft Money and Word for Windows are registered trademarks of
Microsoft Corporation.

Library of Congress Cataloging-in-Publication Data

Perry, Greg M.
   Managing rental properties for maximum profit / Greg Perry.
     p.   cm.
   Includes index.
   ISBN 1–55958–572–2 pbk.
     1. Real estate management — United States. 2. Rental
housing — United States — Management. I. Title.
HD1394.P47   1993
   333.5'068 — dc20   92–42950
                                                      CIP

---

95 96 97 RRD 10 9 8 7 6 5 4 3 2 1

Printed in the United States of America

*This book is only possible because of the
Master Landlord, my father, Glen Perry.
Thanks, Dad, you're the greatest.*

Contents

Acknowledgments

THE PRIMARY CONTRIBUTORS to this book are all the tenants I have had over the years. They continually teach me how to improve my landlording approach. It seems that the more I care about tenants' needs, the better tenants I have. I now believe that good tenants are always out there and it is the responsibility of the landlord to bring out the best in them. Only when landlords provide safe, clean, affordable housing will tenants be the "good" kind that landlords dream about.

Roger Stewart at Prima Publishing is the hands-down winner for caring editors. Roger had patience with me throughout several computer books during the past few years; he still has confidence in my writing abilities on other topics. Roger is almost as responsible for this book as I am because of the freedom he gave me in its content and his unerring judgment on its review. I also want to thank the others at Bookman Productions who turned my manuscript into a decent book, primarily Candace Demeduc.

My greatest friend and mentor, Michael Stapp, has encouraged me through every one of my fifteen books. Michael, because of your encouraging words I often kept writing when I would have otherwise quit.

My family stands behind me the most, and their support is the only reason I have any success in life. My beautiful bride, Jayne, travels around the globe with me and cleans rental properties when we're home. She probably never expected to have such contrasts in her life, but I suspect she is rarely bored. Glen and Bettye Perry, my parents, are the key to my oomph in life. No other son could dream of the support they provide.

To my readers, the landlords and would-be landlords out there (consisting of landlording gentlemen and landlording ladies), I hope you pick up a few skills from this book, adding to the bag of tricks you currently use. Landlording requires energy and patience, but it also includes lots of relaxing time once you streamline your efforts.

Greg Perry

Introduction

SOME READERS WILL pick up this book out of desperation. These frustrated landlords have almost abandoned all hope of enjoying their landlording duties. Other landlords have found ways to put their properties on auto pilot (without hiring a management company, that is) and might want to hone their landlording skills even further. Some readers may not even own rental properties yet they want to know what to expect. Although no book can be all things to all people, this book attempts to help people in the three categories just mentioned: frustrated landlords, happy landlords, and would-be landlords. Whatever your landlording success has or has not been, you will find ample help in this book to start you on the path to easy landlording.

There are other books on the market that offer landlording advice for the big-time landlord, owner of apartment complexes and rental corporations. This book is intended for the small-time landlord, someone who owns only one or a handful of properties. There are just too many individual landlords out there wanting some hands-on advice not to offer them a survivor's landlording manual.

Landlording can be an extremely enjoyable, profitable, and relaxing career. The book you now hold is *teeming* with landlording advice, tips, warnings, and shortcuts. It's not a get-rich, no-money-down, fancy marketing manual but a book of hands-on advice, immediately helpful to anyone who is a landlord or who wants to be one. Exceptionally important advice is set off with a line, so that it will stand out in the book and in your memory.

To achieve landlording success, you must be a *caring* landlord. This book's primary goal is to show you how to streamline your landlording activities while still being the landlord your tenants expect. Too many rental owners are absentee landlords, never seeing their property or spending a dime on its upkeep. However, you can be an absent landlord without being an absentee landlord. This book shows you the many ways you can prepare your properties so that their maintenance is minimal. This book also teaches you how to find good tenants in only a few hours of your time, how to keep them, and how to buy properties that attract them. Most important, this book shows you how to make money without spending a lot on property upkeep or on continued tenant recruitment.

In order to ease into a successful landlording career, you must do your homework. Preparing the rental properly, attracting the best tenants, and buying more properties in the best rental locations are the keys to loving your very part-time job of landlording.

PLEASE SHARE YOUR IDEAS

This is not a finished landlording text by any means. Future revisions will include comments and suggestions made by you, the readers, as you continue to share your experiences with me. Different towns, different homes, and especially different people can provide lots of good material that should be shared with other landlords across the country. I welcome your ideas and suggestions to provide readers of future editions with timely advice on tenant care and the enjoyment of rental property.

If you have your own landlording nightmares, solutions, and shortcuts to share, I would be grateful to hear from you. If your material appears in future editions of this book, you will receive a free copy for your library. Jot down a note on a postcard or letter and mail it to:

Greg Perry
P.O. Box 35752
Tulsa, OK 74153-0752

Please enclose your return address with your correspondence. Thank you in advance for your help. Readers of future editions will benefit from your experiences.

CHAPTER ONE

Getting Good Tenants

THE HAPPIEST LANDLORDS are those with the best tenants. If you've experienced bad times with your rental property, the odds are good that those problems were people oriented; more specifically, those problems were tenant oriented. Bad tenants will make you wish you had never seen that property. Good tenants will help you forget that you are a landlord. Seek good tenants! If waiting for the right tenants means keeping your house vacant for an extra month, then wait. Problems arise when you rent to people who do not meet your income and rental history requirements. You do not want late-night calls from bothersome tenants asking when you will paint their back fence. More important, you want tenants who pay on time and take as much pride in their dwelling as you do.

The first step in becoming a successful landlord is to find responsible tenants. If you have proud tenants, tenants who are reasonable with their requests, and tenants who pay on time, you will enjoy your life as a landlord. Landlords who own rental properties with good tenants have time to acquire several more properties and slowly build their rental empire. Landlords with tenant problems, however, never seem to have time to themselves; they are always dealing with problems that prevent them from enjoying the benefits of property management.

A wise real estate agent once described the three most important factors in selling real estate: (1) location, (2) location, and (3) location. If those are the three most important factors in selling real estate, the three most important factors in renting property, in order of importance, are (1) advertise properly, (2) advertise properly, and (3) advertise properly.

The key to successfully acquiring good tenants is to draw a large pool of potential tenants from which to choose. Good advertising will attract lots of would-be tenants to your property. Once they are there, your job is easier—more people will fulfill your rental requirements than if only a handful wants your place. Do not waste your time and money on unproved advertising methods; by staying with the basics, you will soon have more would-be tenants than any of your competing landlords! This chapter demonstrates how successful landlords advertise effectively and increase the number of good and interested tenants.

Advertising

Getting a tenant is simple. You must advertise in the classified advertising section of your newspaper. No other method consistently proves itself with successful results. There are other ways to advertise, but newspaper advertisement is easy and works best.

Nothing works as well as newspaper advertising.

Some landlords have limited success with other forms of advertising, but their methods are often costly or time-consuming or simply ineffective. For example, instead of advertising in a newspaper, you could place a sign in front of the house that lets drive-bys know it's for rent. But the next day, you'll get a call from neighbors who complain that some crazy kid put your sign in their yard.

Some owners put "For Rent" signs in the front window of their rentals. These signs do not get stolen as easily as those in the front yard. Those crazy kids will probably not even see such a sign, but neither will most of the people who drive past the property. Those who do see it are often in too much of a hurry to stop and read its details.

Besides being ineffective, signs in the yard or window of your property cause safety problems. You should not tell the world that your home is vacant. With a sign, it is obvious. You want to announce the vacancy to as many would-be tenants as possible, but you do not want to invite vandals and vagrants. Granted, an ad in the newspaper clearly labels your house as an empty target, but people scanning those pages are generally interested in finding a home to rent.

You can also pin messages on community bulletin boards or advertise in trading newspapers with the washing machines and used cars. Some landlords with time on their hands (and there aren't many of those) stack fancy flyers on the racks outside of grocery stores. There is nothing inherently wrong with any of these methods. They each get the word out and attract more people than a newspaper advertisement will by itself. Nevertheless, you will probably find that the extra time and energy are just not worth the results.

The time-tested means for the successful landlord is always local newspaper advertising in the "Rentals" classified section. The classifieds are the first place future tenants look. When they do look there, you want to grab their attention at the start and not let go.

THE WORDING OF YOUR NEWSPAPER AD

"How do I word my ad?" is a question asked by many landlords every time a rental falls vacant. The answer is easy: *Put every detail in the ad that the would-be tenant would want to know.* Include the property's address, the number of bedrooms, the air conditioner/heating status (central, forced air, lots of blankets needed, or whatever), garage, carpet, dishwasher, fireplace, the monthly (or weekly) rental amount, the deposit, the pet policy (Do you allow them? How many and what kind?), the children policy (Adults only? How many people can live in the place?), the waterbed policy, and the lease terms (six months, one year, or whatever).

The smart landlord knows that a good ad costs more than a bad one but a good ad produces quicker results. Put yourself in the shoes of a would-be tenant: You know exactly the most money you can pay and you know the smallest house you want to rent. Those two pieces of information are in almost every ad.

For Rent: 3-bedroom, 2-bath house. $575/month, $350 deposit. Call 555-4321.

Consider the ad displayed in this section. It costs very little and seems to tell the would-be tenant everything that he or she needs to know. Would you rent this home if you were a tenant? You cannot answer that. This ad does nothing except raise more questions. Guess who gets to answer those questions, twenty-four hours of the day? That's right, *you* do. This type of ad begs every reader to call you for more information. The only reason every reader will not call (only every other one will) is that half will scan the classifieds until they spot a more informative ad that answers their questions without requiring that they pick up a phone.

The book you now hold strongly urges you to save money in every way you can. Your properties are supposed to be investments, but an investment that loses money is not only a headache but a liability. Nevertheless, the ad is the one place you should spend what it takes to give your readers every necessary detail, so they do not have to call you for information. If a reader must call, both you and the possible tenant are doing more work than necessary.

Comprehensive ads cut down the time you spend with prospective tenants.

TELL THE READER *ALMOST* EVERYTHING

Keep only two details out of that ad: your name and phone number. No matter how thorough you are in your ad's description of the properties, some people will call to ask you something trivial. Even worse, some will ask questions that you already answered in the ad! Stop this at the source by leaving your name and phone number completely *out* of the ad. You can only go so far; once you realistically describe everything about the property, you have done your job.

Don't put your name and number in the ad!

Without your name or phone number, how will your would-be tenants get in touch with you to see the inside of the property? You will show them, of course. Only now you are working smarter than before.

The most time-consuming task of rental properties is answering questions about your ad and showing the property. The day your ad appears in the paper, you may get thirty callers, twenty of them wanting to see the inside of the property. You do not have time to handle all these calls or to show the property twenty separate times.

HOLD AN OPEN HOUSE

The typical rental property owner places an ad in the newspaper that includes his or her phone number. When a prospective tenant calls to see the property, the owner must get in the car to show the home, if that would-be tenant wants to see the house immediately. Invariably, as soon as the owner gets home from one showing, he or she gets another call to show the property again.

In these times of depressed housing markets, owners seem happy to oblige would-be tenants. If a potential tenant wants to see the property at 4:35 in the morning, many owners feel that's better than having to cover another month's mortgage payment!

Despite the housing slump in many areas, you cannot cater to the whims of every caller who wants to see the property. Even though callers are potential renters, if you ever want your rental empire to grow, you do not have time to show the home twenty times to twenty different people.

In place of your name and phone number, put the day and time when you will be at the property to show it. Wouldn't you like to make one trip instead of twenty? This strategy alone will save many landlords tremendous amounts of time and gas starting today.

Hold an open house at a time that is convenient for you and most working people. Successful landlords do not make twenty-five trips to show the home to twenty-five possible tenants. Rather, they make one trip to show the home to twenty-five possible tenants.

Reserve several hours on a Friday afternoon and on Saturday for your property's open house. Between four o'clock and six o'clock on a Friday afternoon lets you catch people who drop by after work. Early Saturday afternoon is also a premium time for home lookers. Whatever time you decide on, be sure to prepare the house for viewing by cleaning it thoroughly and touching up all the details that will catch the lookers' eyes. Chapter 2, "Preparing the Rental Property," describes many things you can do to turn the home into a showcase.

You will have more people see the property during your open house than would have seen it otherwise. Prospective tenants appreciate the fact that they do not have to meet you alone. Because an open house can involve several people, would-be renters can maintain more distance between themselves and you than if you made a special trip to see each one individually. Women who do not want to risk meeting a stranger at an empty house especially appreciate this.

Because you clearly posted the open house hours in your ad, people can fit it into their schedules, instead of trying to negotiate a mutual meeting time. One spouse can drop by after work, then bring the other back if interest is high. But if they have to call you for an individual viewing, the entire family might want to come, perhaps to find that the house is not what they need.

Not only will you draw a larger number of prospective tenants at an open house, not only will you be saved the time and gas of multiple showings, but the *open house's prospective tenants are more interested in your property than the typical prospective renter would otherwise be.* Think back for a minute on the contents of a good, comprehensive ad, which describes everything pertinent about the home. Your ad lets prospective renters know exactly what comprises your property before they ever come to the open house. From the ad, they know that the property's features match their needs. They know the deposit and the terms you expect. They know the address; most of them will have driven by before your open house just to "scope out" the property. They liked what they saw on the outside or they would not be at the open house.

They come to make sure that you honestly described the rental and that it is clean. That's when you grab them—your house will be sparkling. After you finish this book, you will also know all the extras that make people want to rent your property at first sight.

By placing a proper ad and holding an open house, you will find yourself with only two problems:

- What will you do with the extra time on your hands?
- Out of the large number of people who are begging for your property, how will you choose a tenant?

Landlords across the country would *love* to have those problems!

Before moving on, please know that this advice is given to you after years of working and reworking rental property management. Be assured that you will find many good tenants by using these methods. Although there are many other ways of getting good tenants, this is one that proves successful time and time again.

A SAMPLE AD WITH A CATCHY HEADER

Read the effective advertisement for a rental house displayed in this section. You can change the details, but the format should remain basically the same whether you are leasing a home or a duplex in a large city or a small town. Notice the phrase centered in boldface letters at the top. Most newspapers will do this for you at a small extra charge. The reason your ad will stand out is that most owners do not want to spring for that extra line. Competing (and less savvy) landlords will be placing a second ad when you are signing your first lease.

DON'T MISS THIS ONE!

Beautiful, clean, 3-bedroom, 2-bath home, carpeted, dishwasher, laundry hookups, central heat/air, separate dining area, ceiling fans,

miniblinds, fenced backyard, 2-car attached garage, safe neighborhood, 1 outside pet OK, up to 2 children OK, waterbed OK, close to
schools, 6-month lease minimum, $575/month, $350 security/
cleaning refundable deposit. 1013 S. Illinois. Will show this Friday
4–6 P.M. and Saturday 1–3 P.M.

The headline phrase is an attention getter. Put any
catchy two- to four-word expression here, but make sure it
fits well centered across the top of the ad. You might want
to try the following:

- Like New!
- Stable Neighborhood!
- 10 Mins from Downtown!
- Country Living!
- Dream Home!
- BEST DEAL!
- Newly Remodeled!

Do not overdo the advertisement but do succinctly
supply every bit of needed information. Remember, since
you will not put your name or phone number in the ad, you
must inform readers of all the details they will need.

KEEP YOUR AD HONEST

Proudly describe everything pertinent about your
rental property but do not exaggerate or misrepresent it.
Otherwise you will lose trust (and most of your would-be
tenants). As soon as readers see the inside of the property,
they will know whether you told the entire truth.

Many of your ad's readers have been lied to by potential landlords over the years. They will naturally be appre-
hensive and a little mistrusting of you before they see your

rental. Think of their feelings when they find that your ad is one hundred percent correct. If anything, your ad *under-sells* the coziness and pride the home displays. The would-be tenants' trust is impossible to gain after you lose it, so capture trust at the beginning when it is easiest to snare.

Be honest in the ad!

If you can cut costs without sacrificing quality, pass those costs onto your renters by setting your rent levels slightly below that of your competition. But if you currently require higher rent than surrounding properties, make certain that your home is sparkling clean and offers enough differences to warrant the extra rent. This book will show you how to make your rental a showplace. It will no longer be a time-consuming headache but something to be proud of.

Throughout this book, you will find ways to lower your cost of being in the rental business, but the original cost of the home is the primary determinant of the rent you must charge. As you buy more properties (and you will after reading here how easy property management can be), be open to low-cost housing with good structures located in better neighborhoods. Generally, a fix-up home is much cheaper in the long run than a home that is ready to move into, even if you hire someone to make every repair. Chapter 10, "Finding and Buying More Properties," offers lots of advice on finding the perfect low-cost rental property.

This book is not a magic formula for success. But if it does nothing more than teach you to develop your own techniques for money-saving, pride-of-ownership, fully occupied rental properties, its goal is surpassed. The magic comes from your own pride in your property, which will shine through in your ad if you are honest with your readers.

Renters All Over the Place

The combination of newspaper advertisement and open house will find you a good tenant, but there are other avenues to explore as well. The easiest and cheapest advertising you can do is word of mouth. Although it does not reach the large audience that a newspaper does, its benefits are appealing if you target the right people.

Be selective with any word of mouth advertising you do. Your friends and coworkers care about you so tell them of an upcoming vacancy. If a friend or coworker sends you a rental prospect, that person is probably a better candidate than a complete stranger. There is still a risk, but it is smaller.

If you eventually rent the property to your friend's candidate, send a crisp twenty-dollar bill and thank-you card to the friend the very next day. Don't go overboard with the thanks, but quietly let that person know that you are grateful for his or her help. The money does two things: It genuinely shows your appreciation, which is its main function. It also makes it even more likely that the next time you have a vacancy your friend will want to help you find another tenant. Two people searching produces many more potential renters than you by yourself.

Let your friends and coworkers know you have a vacancy. Thank them with a small cash gift if they save you time and money by supplying you with a tenant.

You must still be in control of the rental situation, no matter how good-hearted your friends are. Use common sense. Even though your friend probably has your best interests at heart, only you know who can and cannot rent your property. Follow your guidelines for smoking/non-smoking, minimum income, and so forth. The candidate your friend passes by you should exceed your minimum qualifications for rental, just as a stranger off the street would have to do. In Chapter 3, "Open House and Tenant Selection," you will read some guidelines for selecting tenants in a legal and orderly fashion.

ADVERTISING IN SURROUNDING TOWNS

Rarely will you have to place an ad outside your property's town. A well-written, comprehensive ad attracts renters like nothing else. However, occasionally local economic conditions and timing may be against you. If you hold several open houses but still feel that the candidates do not measure up, consider advertising in surrounding towns for the next week's open house.

Many people work outside their hometowns. You may attract someone who works in the town where your property is but lives farther out and is tired of the commute. Or you may be the answer for a family who wants to get closer to relatives living in your area.

Be cautious about doing too much advertising too early, however. The comprehensive ad with open house will do wonders to improve the number of rental candidates. But if you also place ads in lots of different places the first week or two of advertising, you run a big risk of spending much more than you needed to get a tenant. Even though surrounding areas offer good prospects, most of your lookers will be from the same town as your own property.

Using a Rental Service

Should you consider a rental service? Most landlords consider hiring their job out to another agency several times throughout their property management tenure — especially when a bad tenant slips past all precautions and rents their home. Many real estate companies offer a management service for rental properties. They will advertise, show your home, handle complaints, collect the rent, order the repairs, and send you what is left of the rent (if anything) after they do their job.

There are two drawbacks to using a rental service: The first is loss of income. The property management firm has to make a profit to survive, so it will charge what it needs to maintain its profit margins. Remember that you too have to make a profit to survive. By the time you pay the mortgage, taxes, and insurance, you may not always have enough to pay the rental service; but because you are locked into a contract, you will have to pay. Even when the service does nothing during a certain month, you still have to pay the monthly fee. Most require a percentage of the rent, with additional charges for any and all repairs, advertising, and showing time.

Manage your own properties for maximum profit and control.

More important, you lose contact with and eventual control of your property. Most property management companies offer high-quality rental services. Despite that, nobody takes pride in your own property as much as you do. There is no way to ensure that the rental service will handle all problems to your exact liking. By the time you finish this book, you will see that managing your own properties is easy and cheap and demands an extremely small amount of your time. If you have had lots of problems with managing your properties in the past, you may be willing to pay most or all of your monthly profit to a rental service, but please finish this book before making that decision.

Summary

Successful landlords do not have to make twenty-five trips to show a property to twenty-five potential tenants; they make *one* trip to show the property to all would-be renters at one time. Successful landlords do not put their phone numbers in the ad. Successful and happy landlords know when to place extra ads in surrounding towns.

The rest of this book describes how your own pride in your rental determines your tenants' response to it. A good ad gets tenants to your open house, but your home must sell itself once they're there, because you cannot. The most effective ad in the world will not make up for run-down property. You need to provide a home that tenants will want to live in for many years.

Chapter 2, "Preparing the Rental Property," describes how you can fix up a home for renting, but it does not describe complete renovation; Chapter 11, "Renovating Your Rental Properties," will give you pointers in that area. If you are like most one- and two-property landlords, you probably have a house that is fundamentally ready to rent. You now must make it stand out from the crowd.

CHAPTER TWO

Preparing the Rental Property

AT THE OPEN house, you do not actually show the home; the home shows itself. Most of the people who come will have driven by at least once before. In fact, you invited the readers of the newspaper ad to do so when you included the address—and you *should* hope that they did drive by before coming to the open house. That way, you know that at least they like the outside of the home. Now your job is to make the inside attractive to them as well.

Your open house will give prospective tenants a good or bad first impression—the choice is yours. A good impression of the outside will disappear if the inside is dirty. At the same time, a bad impression of the outside will be hard to reverse, no matter what the inside of the home looks like.

You can do many wonderful and inexpensive things to make lots of people want to rent your house. This chapter focuses on making your home a "must have" for everyone attending the open house. (For advice on how to completely renovate your home, see Chapter 11.) If you've never attracted enough interested prospective tenants in the past, you need to learn how to make your property stand out from the competition. Show those would-be tenants why *your* house should be their future home.

Cleanliness Is Paramount

If you do not make sure that your home is clean for open house, you are in the wrong business. There is no excuse for dirty carpets, walls, counters, or sinks. The only people you want as renters are those who are turned off by dirt in their home.

It's to be hoped that your former tenants left the house in move-in condition. Good tenants will. Nevertheless, some landlords pride themselves on never giving back a cleaning deposit, even to a deserving tenant. They feel that the cleaning deposit is their payment for having to find another tenant. But tenants can challenge these landlords in court. One landlord had a problem on his hands when a savvy tenant who wanted his deposit back took photographs of the clean house along with the daily newspaper to prove the date of the pictures. This landlord had to pay a large penalty to his ex-tenants in addition to the original deposit.

Guests always see dirt; they rarely notice cleanliness.

Don't try to squeeze extra pennies from tenants by keeping their deposits if they leave the home clean. You should always *want* to give back every dime of your tenants' deposit. When you are able to do so because your tenants cleaned the house prior to leaving, your job is made easier. Remember, you want to spend as little time and money as you can to manage your property. When tenants move in, tell them that you want to give them back their cleaning deposit. Tell them you have done so many times with former tenants who took care of the house and left it in as good or better condition as when they moved in. When tenants give notice that they will move out, encourage them to clean up and cheerfully mention that you will return their deposit if they do. No matter how much notice a renter gives, your job is easier and you are out less money in the long run if you have nothing to repair and very little to clean.

At the open house, every spot on the wall, every piece of lint on the carpet, and every fingerprint on the faucets will stand out in the potential renters' eyes — and you do not want tenants who care little about cleanliness! If would-be tenants want to move into a clean home, they are more likely to keep it that way. Be wary of people who want to rent the home virtually sight unseen. Typically, these people have bad rental histories, and they're taking advantage of the fact that some landlords have problems finding renters (you should no longer consider yourself one of those).

Whether or not the former tenants left the house clean, you must take responsibility to make sure everything is ready for immediate occupancy. Take pride in the job you do. This is your property! When you begin to look at your rental as a problem, you lose interest and your attitude shows to potential tenants. But when you see your home as an investment, as only a minor time-consumer (it can be), and as your second home if needed (you never know), you will go the extra mile to prepare the home for showing. You want top-quality renters. You want to lure the best renters away from the huge apartment complexes and the corporate landlords. You have the ability to do so, and the first step begins with a broom.

Take with you everything you need to clean the house so you do not have to make extra trips (to like landlording you must spend as little time doing it as possible). Below is a list of cleaning supplies you should take with you to spruce up the home for open house:

vacuum	furniture polish (for wood-
broom	work, cabinets, doors,
mop	baseboards)
bucket	spare light bulbs

rags, sponges, towels
cleaners, disinfectants
glass cleaner
toilet bowl brush
rubber gloves
trash bags

smoke alarm batteries
touch-up paint
common tools (screwdrivers, wrench, hammer, nails)

If you have more than one rental, it may be more convenient to keep the needed cleaning supplies and equipment in a ready-to-go box. This will save you the time of gathering these items when you need to clean one of your rentals.

Disinfect all toilets, baths, and sinks. Let bleach stand in any white porcelain that has discolored. If bleach does not take off the dingy color, you may have to purchase a stain remover for the job. Many landlords replace worn-out porcelain sinks with stainless steel sinks, which clean easily and do not discolor.

If you have difficulty removing stains from the toilet bowl, chances are good that mineral deposits have built up over the years. The only solution is to rough them off. First, drain the bowl by turning off the water and flushing the toilet. Sprinkle pumice powder on the stains and rub with a hard brush (but not one with steel bristles) or a coarse rag. You will not mar the surface of the bowl, but you will remove the stains after a little effort. Mineral build-up is common in older toilet bowls, especially ones that have not been used in a while.

If your house has a garbage disposal, run a lemon through it before each open house. This replaces any unfresh odors that may be living in the drain with a pleasant aroma.

Remember to put fresh air filters in the air conditioner/heating unit. These filters need to be replaced about every two to three months. Most people go much longer than that between replacements. Dirty filters make the units work harder, the home will not heat or cool as fast, and your tenants will have higher utility bills and less money when the rent comes due. By changing the filters when you prepare the house for showing, you gain two or three months before you have to change them again. Better yet, buy a few extra and leave them in the house. They are very inexpensive and are often available even cheaper in two-for-one sales. Show the new tenants how to change the filter to keep their bills low.

Frequently replace the filters on your heater and air conditioner.

CHECK THE DETAILS

Make sure every door and window opens and closes easily and quietly. A sticky door quickly gets torn away from its hinges by opening and closing it. Make sure the locks lock. Make sure windows stay up when opened. Check for air leaks under outside doors and windows. A bead of caulking around a window seal and an insulating strip at the bottom of a door improve the home's soundproofing and air efficiency. Check the doors and windows even if they were fine the last time the rental was vacant; caulking can dry up and weather stripping can come loose.

You will do your renters a favor if you put window screens on the windows. They can turn off the air conditioning and enjoy the spring and fall without getting bitten by insects coming through screenless windows. Uniform-looking screens improve the appearance of the outside of the home as well.

Window screens are not expensive. You can often find like-new screens at junkyards, but brand-new screens are inexpensive as well. Be sure to measure each window before you go to the store, since windows in a house vary in size. If the existing screens are coming loose, you can buy splicing and a screen repair roller. (Chapter 11 describes screen repair in more detail.)

This might be a touchy subject, but make sure ample toilet paper is in every bathroom. Guests may need the toilet paper when you show the house. Some people will ask to use the bathroom when they come to the open house and if you do not let them, be assured they will not rent the home.

Remove kitchen and bathroom odors first by thoroughly cleaning with a lemon-based disinfectant. Unless you clean the offending surfaces, you can only temporarily hide the odors. After cleaning, a room deodorizer will help freshen the scent — but do not purchase a strongly scented one. To some sensitive noses, that would be worse than the original problem. Sprinkle carpet freshener into the carpet before you vacuum. It does wonders.

The home should smell good as well as look clean.

If you supply a refrigerator (and you should because renters usually do not carry one around), put a fresh box of baking soda in it; pour the old box down the sink to freshen the drain. Almost everyone at the open house will open the refrigerator. Because renters are used to seeing soiled, smelly refrigerators with cracked shelves in the houses of other landlords, surprise your prospective tenants with the fresh clean look and smell of your refrigerator.

Some landlords understandably like to minimize utility bills when their rental is vacant. If you choose to turn off the refrigerator during the house's vacancy, prop the door open. Even a clean refrigerator will produce mildew and begin to smell if left off and closed for more than several days.

Patch large nail holes in the walls and clean or paint over dirty spots on the walls and baseboards. Every distraction of would-be tenants' eyes registers as a negative.

UTILITIES WHILE VACANT

Keep the basic utilities on while you prepare your rental for showing. You must have water and electricity to clean the home properly. During the winter months, keep the heat on as well. This keeps the pipes from freezing while nobody is there to keep the place warm.

Heat tape is imperative for cold-winter conditions.

In cold-winter areas, have a plumber or electrician install heat tape on the water pipes in the crawl space (if the home has one). Heat tape has wires that connect to an electrical source. When the temperature falls below a certain value, the heat tape charges and warms the pipes so they do not freeze and burst (a broken water pipe is extremely costly and never fun to repair).

A good thing about heat tape is that it works whether you are there or away as long as you keep the electricity turned on. When tenants move in, the heat tape continues to work, even if they go out of town during a cold spell.

When a tenant vacates your property, you must get the utilities turned on in your name as soon as possible. The sooner they are on, the sooner you can prepare the home for showing and the sooner the rent will roll in.

You will have to grit your teeth and pay the utility companies' hook-up fees. Most utilities do not actually turn service off and on, but they do need to send a meter reader out to get a final reading for the previous tenant so they can transfer the billing to your name. Nobody likes to pay for this but the utility companies must pass the cost to someone.

Many utilities now offer a leave-on service designed specifically for landlords. When you sign up for leave-on service, you tell the utility company the location of your property (or properties). When the company receives a shut-off notice from the former tenant, it automatically transfers the service to your name. The utility company charges you less for this service than it would if you called each time to request a transfer. Not only is it cheaper but, during the winter months, the home will remain heated even if the tenants quietly move out without your knowledge.

If you sign up for the leave-on policy, your only responsibility is to inform the utility company whenever a new tenant moves in. You do not want to pay for the new tenant's electric and gas any longer than you have to. As soon as you call, the utility company will stop billing you for future usage and will transfer the subsequent charges to the new tenant after they verify occupancy.

Take care of the heating element on an electric water heater.

If the home is all-electric, or if you simply have an electric water heater, you must leave the water on all the time that the electricity is on. Although this is not a safety danger, the heating element will burn up if the tank is allowed to go dry. A plumber or electrician can replace the heating element, but you do not want the bill—especially since the problem is so easy to avoid.

To be safe and to avoid unnecessary utility bills, turn off the breaker to the electric water heater as soon as you finish cleaning. You do not need hot water to show the house. In addition, if the electricity goes off while the house is still vacant, the heating element will remain intact.

Finally, leave on some lights, both inside and out, while the home is vacant. A dark house invites problems.

HIRING CLEANING HELP

Every landlord considers paying someone else to do all the cleaning and fix-up work. Although this book attempts to show you how to manage your properties on your own, without relying on outside services and spending lots of money, there are times when hiring others makes sense.

You might first consider "hiring" your own family. Involve your spouse and children if they are willing. Pay your children to run the vacuum and wipe the walls. Promise your spouse an extravagant present if he or she helps! Whatever you do, make the property's work upbeat and fun. Take a portable television or radio with you. At noon, take your family for a lunch-break pizza party. This is their property too, and their future partly depends on its rentability.

If you have no family, or if your family cannot help, consider hiring others to clean, paint, and prepare the home for occupancy. The work is tax deductible to you as the owner of the home. Even more important, the job will be done faster than you by yourself, and the income can begin sooner.

For example, there are lots of house-cleaning services that use their own supplies and equipment. They can be in and out of your house faster than you would be able to clean the half-bathroom yourself. They are well-trained and know how to make a home shine in record time. Given that their payment is tax deductible and that they work so fast, you should never rule them out.

The key is to let others do what they do best while you continue to do what you do best. Eventually you will rent to high-quality, paying tenants, if you manage your property well, inspect the details, ensure cleanliness, attend to the extras, prepare for the open house, and do all the other tasks needed to make sure things run smoothly. If you like to clean, paint, or whatever, certainly do so. The money saved is nice, and more important, you develop an increased sense of pride in your property. However, even do-it-yourselfers need to hire help now and then.

Safety First

You, your insurance agent, and your tenant will be happier if you purchase at least two smoke alarms. If you own a two-story house, be sure to get at least one for each floor. Make sure that each bedroom door is close to a smoke alarm. There is no excuse to forget smoke alarms, and you open yourself up to a lot of liability if there ever is a fire.

When preparing the house for showing, be sure to check the batteries in the smoke alarms. Electric alarms do not require batteries, but they must be installed by an electrician. Battery smoke alarms have test buttons that demonstrate the battery's life. Even if the battery is still good, replace it if it's been a while since you last did so.

Place a five-pound all-purpose fire extinguisher under the kitchen sink.

A fire extinguisher in the kitchen may be the best investment you can make. Put it under the kitchen sink. Every time you prepare your home for showing, check the extinguisher's gauge to make sure it is fully charged.

Resist the temptation to "test" the fire extinguisher by shooting it. Instead, rely on the gauge. If you shoot an extinguisher, even for a short burst, the pressure will slowly leave it over the next week or so. If you do not use it, the extinguisher will remain fully charged for several years.

If the fire extinguisher has been in the home for a year or so, gently shake it to mix the contents a little. Although shaking is not required, it's recommended to keep the contents from settling on the bottom.

If the gauge shows that the pressure is gone from the extinguisher, replace it with a new one. Although many extinguishers can be recharged, the cost of recharging is almost as high as a new purchase, especially for small home extinguishers. Besides, the contents of new extinguishers are fresher and they tend to hold their charge better than older ones that have been recharged.

Smoke alarms and fire extinguishers are a lot like insurance; you hope they are a waste of money and that you never have to use them.

Every time you walk in and around your vacant house, look for loose carpet, weak door hinges, sagging flooring, loose stair steps, exposed wiring, and anything else that might pose a danger to tenants. Each house has a different layout and a different set of potential problems.

Fasten loose wires to walls and baseboards.

If the cable TV wire or phone cord is loose, buy a package of U-shaped staple tacks to secure the wiring along a wall. However there are materials (such as Formica) that cannot be nailed or tacked to. A few drops of clear glue along the wire, temporarily held against the wall with tape, will secure the wire in place.

If you own a two-story home or townhouse, make sure the stair railings are secure. If you need to install a handrail, buy a kit at a home improvement store.

Your tenants will recognize that you take safety seriously. This adds to your image as a caring landlord, and the better renters will appreciate your style. You are showing that you care about them and the home. Landlords who do not maintain their properties and who do not limit hazards around the house often attract tenants who have the same low concern for the property.

The Extras Make Your Rental Attractive

No matter how good or bad your area's rental market is, you are in constant competition with other landlords trying to rent to good people. You must make your home stand apart from the crowd. You are in business and the renters are your customers. You must attract better quality, long-term, paying renters away from other landlords.

You might be surprised by how little it takes to make the home attractive to renters. By adding inexpensive extras to the house, you draw more would-be tenants to your open houses. Whether your rent is slightly lower or higher than your competition (it should never be much different from a competing house, but remember that lower rent attracts more would-be renters), the property will speak for itself if you go the extra mile to distinguish your place from the others.

The key to owning and managing rental properties is to minimize your time and effort. To achieve this, you must invest a little extra effort up front, when preparing the home to show it, thereby attracting the best renters you can find. Spend as much time as necessary to turn the property into a clean, well-kept, welcome attraction to renters. The more renters you attract, the higher the minimum income and rental history standards you can set and the fewer problems you will have down the road.

CARPETS MAKE THE HOME

You must vacuum the carpets and spot clean them where needed. Steam clean the entire carpet if the soil and stains warrant it. When tenants look at your carpet, they are not checking for dirt, although they will always see it if it is there. They are picturing themselves and their children lying on pillows on the floor in front of the television set.

Your rental will have no appeal if the carpet is not clean. Depending on the age of the house, the rent you are asking, and the time since your last renovation, your carpet might not be brand-new, and it doesn't need to be. But it *must* be clean, which is much more important to renters than the carpet's age.

Of course, if your carpet shows lots of signs of wear, or if it is too dated, you should consider replacing it. When you buy carpet, look for traditional style and color. A nonsculptured, small nap, light-tan carpet is always appropriate and always goes with any tenant's furniture.

Look around for bulk discounts on carpet. especially if you have more than one rental property. Ask the carpet company's manager if you can find a durable style and color for a good price. If the manager will sell at a discount, buy more than you need. You will eventually use it.

Replacing worn-out carpet will improve the rentability of your home by three hundred percent.

After a while, every rental unit you own should have the same carpet. Think about the advantages of such consistency: If you ever need to replace the carpeting in a room or a portion of a room (such as in a closet where the carpet was soiled beyond cleaning by oily shoes), you will have a matching remnant.

Carpet does not have to be expensive to have a nice look and feel. Your tenants are much more interested in its cleanliness than in its cost or stylishness.

If you have more than one rental property, consider buying a carpet cleaning machine or cleaning attachments for your vacuum.

Clean the carpet after each occupant. The fresh smell and the uniform look of the nap will help attract new tenants. The sooner you get new tenants into a vacant home, the faster your pocketbook fills up.

CEILING FANS PAY FOR THEMSELVES

Install a ceiling fan in each bedroom and living area. Purchase fans with ample lighting so your tenants will be comfortable with the lights. Short-sighted landlords cringe at the thought of buying two or three ceiling fans for each rental house. But ceiling fans make a great first impression because they help to fill the empty rooms. And tenants realize they can use the fans rather than the air conditioner on days that are merely warm rather than sweltering (ceiling fans cool rooms by approximately seven degrees).

Buy a ceiling fan that offers reverse motion. During the cold months, a backwards spin helps distribute warm air in the room.

Most inexpensive ceiling fans have attractive wooden or wicker blades. Many allow you to put different material on each side of the blade so you can get the look you want. These days, for a reasonable price at most home improvement or department stores, you can purchase attractive ceiling fans, with bronze or brass light kits, that will last for years.

Choose a ceiling fan appropriate to the size of the room. The number of blades (three, four, or five) really doesn't matter, but their width does. Typical sizes are listed below:

Fan Blade Size	Room Size
42 inches	up to 100 square feet
52 inches	100 to 400 square feet
56 inches	over 400 square feet

Hang the fan eight to twelve inches from the ceiling. Anything closer will not allow the air to circulate properly.

Get a sturdy ladder and someone to help you hang your first ceiling fan. Before you start, make sure you flip the main breaker off or disconnect the fuses for the house. The first ceiling fan you install will be the most difficult; you will have no trouble with the rest. The instructions are easy to follow.

The only problem you might experience with a ceiling fan is noise. Every once in a while, you will install a fan that makes a rubbing noise as it spins. There are several things you can do to stop the noise. The first and easiest is to tape a quarter to the top of each blade, one at a time. If a blade is unbalanced, a quarter on the offending blade (or the one opposite to it, depending on the problem) will quiet the fan.

If the quarter does not work, you may not have hung the fan's body vertically on its bracket. A bubble balance will let you know whether the fan is exactly vertical. You may have to remove the cover that hides the hole in the ceiling to make sure you've hung the fan according to the instructions.

If you simply cannot stop the noise, completely remove the fan and rehang it. Although this is an extreme solution—and rarely needed—it might do the trick if all else fails. Only after rehanging the fan a *second* time should you take it back to the store for a replacement.

MINIBLINDS INCREASE THE VISUAL VALUE

Miniblinds spruce up the home's windows; they last for years, help conserve energy, and look great. Because most renters will not hang drapes in windows that already have miniblinds, the window frames will not get full of holes from cheap curtain rods (that never stay up well anyway).

Along with a clean, neutral carpet and ceiling fans, miniblinds impress your would-be renters. Not only do miniblinds look good, they sound even better in your newspaper rental advertisement (not many landlords will bother to install miniblinds; those that do will not think to put them in the ad).

Miniblinds are inexpensive at department stores and are adjustable for a range of window sizes. Be sure to take your window measurements with you when you shop. You will not find heavy-duty, designer miniblinds in a wide range of colors at a department store, but you don't want those anyway. Choose a neutral color, like cream.

Installing miniblinds is similar to installing ceiling fans—it's easy after the first one. If you mess up on your first attempt, chalk it up to experience.

Once you see a room's windows covered by mini-blinds, you will wonder why you never thought of them before. You may even want them in your own home if you don't already have them. They always look neat, they open and close easily, and they allow you to let in (or keep out) varying degrees of light.

The Outside Produces the Real First Impression

Monitor the outside of your home as carefully as the inside. Only if the outside is clean and tidy will people come back for your open house. When you prepare the home for showing, take along trash bags and put in them every piece of trash you find around the outside of the house.

Cut the lawn. You do not necessarily have to edge or get rid of all the weeds, but the lawn should look mowed and be neat. Clean any dirty windows, repair holes in the screens, and make sure that working light bulbs are in the front and back porch light fixtures. (Leave these turned on for security while the home is vacant.)

If your property has a garage, clean it thoroughly. When you show the house, interested renters *will* want to look in the garage. If a previous tenant left any oil on the floor, a bag of generic cat litter will absorb it; you can then sweep it up. Throw away old tires and anything else not nailed down. Your new tenants will want an empty garage with as much room as possible for their cars and for storage.

USE CONSISTENT COLORS

If needed, touch up the exterior with an outside-grade paint. Not only will your home look better, but the paint will help protect and extend the life of the wood. Light trim on a darker colored home is generally *much* more appealing than dark trim on a lighter home. Lighter trim increases your home's visual size by widening the look of the front.

Paint every house the same color.

If you have more than one rental property, try to paint each the same color. This theme of *consistency* prevails throughout this book. The best color to paint your rental house is the same color you paint your own home. As you add properties to your rental empire, paint them the same color too.

This tip alone will save you time and money. Whenever you need to touch up paint, you will always have an extra gallon in your garage. You might even consider buying it in bulk. With each house the same color, you will use it up over a period of several years, especially if you continue to purchase more rentals.

This same advice holds true for the inside of the house. You do not have to paint everything in the house — the trim, walls, and baseboards — the very same color, but whatever color scheme you choose should be your choice for every home you own. Your renters will not know that every house is painted the same and it does not matter if they do. You will probably not have two houses right next to each other.

Being able to touch up paint and match the color at any time is a wonderful maintenance improvement. If you now have one or more houses painted different colors, choose which color you like best. The next time you paint another house, use that color. You will be glad you did.

SHUTTERS IMPROVE THE APPEARANCE

A pair of white plastic shutters costs very little, *never* needs painting, takes eight minutes to install, and *immediately* makes the home look larger and friendlier. If you have a rental home without shutters, put them up now. You do not need them on the back windows, but place them on the front and on any side windows that are visible from the street.

Before you install shutters, stand back and take a good look at the outside of the home. After putting them up, look again. You will think you are looking at a different house. The need for shutters cannot be overemphasized, and yet many people would never think to put them on a rental house.

Plastic shutters last longer than wood shutters and need no maintenance.

Plastic shutters have a wood-grain texture. You can install them with an electric drill and six sheet-metal screws (one in each corner and two in the middle). Select white shutters. They will go with any color you ever paint the house, and they make white house trim come alive, especially on houses with a cream-yellow or colonial-blue background.

There will be times when the effort you put into a rental house is reflected in your own home. One landlady thought the shutters looked so good on her rental house that she went out and bought some for the home she lived in. However, she fell into a trap common to owners. She bought the most expensive wood shutters the store had to offer, because she didn't want to put the cheap plastic shutters on her own home.

But after one of the shutters continually fell from its weight and the wind, and after painting the shutters twice in two years, she had them ripped off and replaced with the same cheap plastic shutters on her rental home. She has never had a shutter problem since. One more item: Not one of her guests has ever, to her knowledge, walked up and knocked on a shutter to see whether it was plastic or wood. Nobody knows or cares whether you have cheap plastic or expensive wood shutters, but *you* will appreciate the plastic ones for many years to come.

The idea is not only that your rental properties should be important to you. If you treat your properties as well (although maybe not always as expensively) as you do your own home, you will attract better tenants—and better tenants take care of a home longer and cause fewer problems for you.

FLOWERS DRAW MORE RENTERS THAN BEES

The day before your newspaper ad appears, buy potted flowers from the local discount store. Plant them in the ground in front of the home, or in attractive plastic outdoor planters, if you have a condo or apartment. You do not have to be a flower expert to cover a small area with color. You also do not have to maintain them. Good tenants will take care of the flowers once they move in.

Don't spend a lot of money on the flowers. But do buy one bag of soil and some peat moss to put around the plants. This shows that you put some care into the outside (even though it took little time and money).

Summary

Of course, cleanliness is necessary. If you follow the advice in this book — and more important, if you learn to develop your own rental improvements and shortcuts — most of your tenants will leave the home cleaner and in better shape than when they moved in.

Beware of the attitude: It's only a rental house, why should I put more effort or money into it? The effort you put into your rental property is an investment, and it's a good one. Put effort into making that home livable, clean, and safe. Put effort into finding good tenants who will take care of the home and who can pay the bills. Your tenants will only be as proud of your home as you are. The effort you put in up front and the money you invest in mini-blinds and all the other extras will result in a house that is easy to rent to tenants who will stay a long time. Over the years, you will have fewer phone calls, fewer expenses, and a happier life of landlording.

Your tenants will *love* renting your house! They will live in a clean, like-new (but maybe actually old) home in which everything works. They will like their quiet neighborhood (the only kind you should buy in). And you will let them know they can call you and get respect. Most important, they will know that you are proud of your property and that you expect them to be proud of it as well.

CHAPTER THREE

Open House and Tenant Selection

YOUR RENTAL IS now ready for open house. You have cleaned the carpet, scrubbed the sinks, put up the shutters, installed the miniblinds, and checked the appliances. You have made the home a showplace. When the time comes for open house, arrive early, turn on enough lights to brighten the rooms, and open an outside door for several minutes to freshen the air. Then begin to welcome the guests.

You do not have to be the world's most outgoing individual to present a good first impression. Remember, people are there to see the house — you are their secondary concern. Make them comfortable and answer their questions, but stay out of their way and do not come on too strong. If you have prepared the home properly, it will sell itself. When the lookers are ready for the next step, be there to hand them rental applications and to describe your expectations of tenants.

This chapter focuses on the open house and also explains how to select tenants. After the open house, you should be left with a stack of applications. You must sift through the applicants in a fair and legal manner, attempting to find the best qualified for your home.

During Open House

During your open house, you must be aware of many things. Be friendly to your guests but not overly pushy. Keep an eye on children without seeming to dislike them (you would be surprised what damage two running children can do!). If your property has outside stairs, make sure they are free from obstacles that could make people fall.

If the weather is snowy or rainy, place doormats both outside and in. You do not want the first looker to soil the carpet, because this will reflect on you no matter how often you explain it.

Thank everyone as they leave, even those who seemed to take no interest in your property. This is basic courtesy; you should respect all who took the time to attend the open house. In addition, a little friendliness on your part might win people over who are on their way to see another property with a landlord not as nice as you. As they leave, tell them about the next open house date (if you plan one or feel there is a chance you will need one) and wish them well in their house hunting.

As prospective tenants view the home, answer all their questions as fully and truthfully as you can. These people need to know as much as possible about the house to make a wise decision. This may be their home for the next few years and the more interested they are in it, the more they will want to know about it.

Show copies of past utility bills that represent typical high- and low-usage months.

Ask the previous tenants or the local utility companies to give you copies of a few utility bills for summer and winter. When you fixed up the home for rent (you will find lots of improvement tips in Chapter 11), you made sure there was adequate insulation, and the utility bills will demonstrate this. If your home is in close competition with another, the lower utility bills may make the difference.

The Rental Application

You may be surprised at the number of landlords who select tenants without using rental applications. These landlords have only vague criteria for renting, usually coming down to who wants it first or who has the most expensive clothes or the flashiest car. There are several problems in choosing rentals this way. You run the risk of renting to someone with inadequate (or no) income, or even worse, with a poor rental history (property damage, drugs, and so on). The most critical problem is the legality of such a system.

Smart landlords take precautions against legal headaches. This book is not a substitute for a good attorney, but it has lots of advice for avoiding legal problems. You open yourself up to discrimination lawsuits if you do not set rental standards, follow those standards, and show proof that you did so.

The rental applications that you require of potential renters help show that you were fair and impartial when you finally decided upon a tenant. You may never be called into court for discrimination, but if you are, a stack of applications goes a long way toward showing how you made your choice.

Keep all rental applications for at least two years.

It is possible (and recommended) to discriminate legally, as long as you show that you were fair across all applicants. You know that you cannot discriminate on the basis of race, creed, religion, or physical impairment. If you do, you will almost certainly be challenged at some point in your landlording career, and you will be hard-pressed to defend such a claim.

There are other forms of discrimination that are not as severe and are perfectly legal. The rental application can supply the information you need to make a final decision based on these other factors. You will need to decide how many, if any, pets you allow the tenant. If you allow pets, you can limit the size and breed. You can suggest no children (your ad should read "Prefer adult tenants only"), but you cannot discriminate against them. You can, however, place a limit on the number of people living in the house (two per bedroom is a standard maximum). You can require that a tenant net or gross a certain level of income before you will rent the property. Many landlords require an income of two or three times the monthly rent. Smoking, past criminal problems, and rental recommendations are legitimate considerations as well.

As a rule of thumb, guard against anything and everything the law specifically states is discrimination and be fair and consistent about the other requirements you impose. You will find the best advice on discrimination at your local library, where you can look at a copy of your state's Landlord and Tenant Act (all fifty states either have such a statute or follow a neighboring state's policy).

Go to the library and copy your state's Landlord and Tenant Act.

Some landlords do not rent to unmarried couples. This policy has been upheld by courts. However, if you follow this policy, you will have a difficult time justifying why you rented to two women or two men the following week. Because families seem more secure and stable, most landlords would like to have them as tenants. But in this day and age, a family is not always going to be available. A fenced-in backyard (and allowing a dog or cat) attracts more families than an open backyard. The cost of the fence is repaid by the stability of the tenants over the years.

If you do rent to unmarried couples or to two people of the same sex, each tenant on the lease should qualify individually. If one of them does not qualify, that person cannot live in your house. In fact, if one does not qualify, then the couple does not either, because a lease is inseparable. Too often, one of the parties decides to split, leaving the other with the lease and the rent payments. Both parties are equally responsible; you have full legal recourse to go after whoever is left holding the rent for the full amount of the lease.

Figure 3-1 shows a sample rental application that works well. Adjust the application to suit the needs of your own property. Tell each applicant to fill in all the blanks that apply. Take plenty of applications and pencils with you to your open house.

Let the applicants know that they can either fill out the application on the spot or they can fill it out later and bring it back. Those applicants who are in a hurry can relax, since they don't have to fill out the application immediately. Also, many people will not have with them all the information you request. You should consider bringing a local telephone book with you to help applicants find phone numbers. This makes your job easier later.

Letting lookers take the application with them also gives an easy out to those people who cannot afford your rental, who do not like it, or who were just looking around to test the waters. They will not feel obligated to apply. Many will take an application and never return it; you might not want to rent to them anyway. People with lousy rental histories rarely want you to know about their

Figure 3-1.   *A sample rental application.*

** Application For Rent **

1013 SOUTH ILLINOIS, MIAMI, FLORIDA 41127

** PERSONAL INFORMATION **

Name: _____   Social Sec. #: _____

Phone: _____   Address: _____   How long? _____

Landlord: _____   Phone: _____   Rent: $_____

Previous address: _____   Landlord: _____

Phone: _____   Previous rent: $_____   How long? _____

Pets? _____   How many, what kind? _____   Smoker? ___

List names of each person who will live here:

_____

Emergency name and phone: _____

** WORK INFORMATION **

Occupation: _____   Present employer: _____   How long? _____

Gross income: $_____   Supervisor: _____   His/her phone: _____

Previous employer: _____   Supervisor there: _____

Other sources of income: _____

** BANKING INFORMATION **

Savings bank and acct. #: _____   Checking acct. #: _____

Credit card: Type: _____   Acct. #: _____

Credit Reference: Name: _____   Acct. #: _____

** AUTOMOBILE INFORMATION **

Car makes: _____   Models: _____   Years: _____

Financed with: _____

*** The above statements are accurate. By signing this application, I authorize reference disclosure for purposes of leasing the property at the address listed above.

Signature: _____   Date: _____

Note: ID is required when you finish this application. This speeds the process and guards against possible problems later.

former landlords. These people are looking for the land-lord who does not ask for references.

Most lookers will probably fill out the application at the open house. Many will want to rent your home and will have no problem applying then and there. As they turn in the applications, you must ask for one more item: You must check their identification to make sure the application matches the applicant. State on the application that you will do this (as Figure 3-1 shows) so they will not be surprised. Pleasantly explain to them that you trust them, but occasionally people fill out an application falsely, for someone completely different with a good credit history (such applications check out but the renters end up not being able to pay).

Request identification with each application turned into you.

As you meet people and collect applications, you will make some initial judgments (but do not make a final decision until you verify the applications). If you feel that certain candidates can pass your minimum require-ments, casually tell them before they leave that you need everyone who will be on the lease to see the home before you make a final rental decision. This will typically be a spouse or a roommate. More than once, one-half of a couple wants the home, but after you cancel the next day's open house and the newspaper ad, the other half, who sees the house later, doesn't want it. If you can get both people to the property during open house, and if both of them like the place, your chances of landing them are strengthened.

Meet all responsible parties before renting.

CHECKING THE APPLICATION

Most landlords do not subscribe to a credit-checking agency, because it is cost-prohibitive unless you pass the charge onto each interested looker. The general rental market is very competitive and your tenants will not want to pay for a credit check except in high-demand areas. If you feel you must subscribe to a credit-checking service, you will have to pass the cost onto the prospective tenants. Many will not pay the credit-check fee. Ease the burden of those who are interested by refunding the fee to the applicant to whom you rent.

Even if you do not subscribe to a credit-checking service, your applicants have no idea whether or not you do; most people are fairly honest on their applications anyway. However, if you are good friends with a real estate agent or a banker, he or she may be able to perform a credit check for you, but do not count on it. Typically, they must have a valid reason to request a credit report, and a favor for a friend is difficult to justify.

The most important information that applicants supply is their previous rental history. No matter how good their income is, or how small their expenses are, their former landlord is the best reference possible. He or she should tell you whether the tenants paid on time and whether they left the home in good, clean order.

If applicants hesitate to give you their current landlord's name and number, that does not always signal that they are bad renters. Actually, good tenants feel bad that they are leaving their landlord; they don't want to "break the news" until they know for sure that they have another place. Explain to the applicants that you will only request a "credit check" from their current landlord, without indicating that it is a check for a new rental.

There are unscrupulous landlords who always give excellent references to their bad tenants. This practice gets the tenants out of their property faster. Be aware this may happen. The selection of a tenant is not a science and you must weigh several factors.

Driving by the applicants' current residence will tell you a little about how they take care of it. If your tenants are supposed to mow their own yard, you will get an idea of how well they would stay on top of mowing. A car or two up on blocks will show you what your property would turn into.

Call the applicant's employer to make sure the applicant has worked as long and in the capacity stated on the application. Not all employers give salary information, but you can ask whether the salary specified on the application is "within range." The longer that applicants have worked in their current company, the more stable they are. Be sure to ask for the payroll department or the primary payroll clerk. Many an employee has been embarrassed when his or her salary information was leaked by the person who happened to answer the credit-check phone call.

Call the applicant's bank to ensure the account information is correct. Ask the bank to tell you how long the account has been open. Generally, banks will not give specific balances over the phone, but they will verify account numbers and will usually tell you the age of the account. Be sure to verify any loans the applicant told you about and ask whether there are any others.

You have no way to verify a lot of the information on the application, but ask for it just the same. Although applicants might leave a few lines blank, usually they'll try to be as complete as possible, especially if they like your rental and have a good credit history. The good news is that better tenants fill out more complete applications—they have less to hide!

It is extremely difficult to compute an applicant's net income. You should base your minimum income levels on gross income unless you have access to a credit-reporting agency with very accurate records. Most applicants will underestimate their expenses without intending to lie, because it is difficult to remember every little expense. About the best you can hope for is a good gross income and a responsible tenant.

If two or more applicants have adequate rental histories and both seem equally well qualified to rent your property, rent to the one who applied the earliest to show that you were impartial. This is not a law, but everything you can do to avoid legal hassles is wise, and the first-come rule further shows your impartiality. Be sure to call the other well-qualified applicants to let them know your decision and tell them you would like to keep their applications on file for a while. Ask them whether you may call them if the chosen applicant decides against renting the home or the next time a vacancy comes up.

Keep all of that vacancy's applications together, even after deciding on a tenant (the date on each application will show the time period). You want to have a full record of each candidate's application. On the top application in the stack, attach a page that explains your rental policy and the selection criteria (the minimum income level and so forth) that you used during that application period.

Keep rental applications at least two years.

Do not feel obligated to hold the second day's open house if you select a tenant from the first day's applicants. You would waste your time as well as that of the people who walk through the house. A small sign in the window saying "Sorry, but this home is already rented" takes care of the lookers the next day. Be sure to cancel your newspaper ad as soon as you inform the new tenant of your decision.

Although your new tenants will probably have to give notice to their present landlord, if they have not done so already, you must get a deposit from them to hold the home as soon as you can. When you inform applicants that you have selected them, ask to meet with them to get the deposit and discuss the lease. The applicants do not actually have to sign the lease then, but you can go over some of the lease's details when you get the deposit. You will need to agree on the exact terms of the lease (the day of move-in, the day rent is due, and so forth) before you can write the lease.

THE DEPOSIT DISCUSSION

Explain to the new tenants that the deposit means you will hold the home for them and rent it to nobody else. However, also explain that the deposit is nonrefundable *if they back out of the deal*. Once the lease goes into effect, the deposit will become their refundable security/cleaning deposit; but until they sign the lease, the deposit is for your mutual protection. The deposit keeps you from renting to someone else and keeps them from backing out of the deal they agreed to.

Get a full deposit immediately after choosing a tenant.

The sooner you get the deposit and agree to the details of the lease, the sooner you will rest easy that another job is almost done. Wait to get the actual deposit in your hands before telling the other applicants you rented the home; in case the tenant and the deposit fall through, you will still have a back-up applicant. Of course, courtesy dictates that you do not keep people waiting more than a day or two for your decision.

Place the deposit in a special *escrowed* account. This tip alone awards more court judgments in the favor of the landlord than any other thing you can do. The deposit your tenant gives you is *not your money*. You cannot spend it for any reason until the tenant moves out and violates the lease's deposit description. Be sure to specify that the deposit is for *cleaning and security*. If you do not specify this, tenants can claim it is a cleaning *or* a damage deposit *only* (they will choose the opposite of the one they violated).

Don't pocket the deposit; hold it in escrow.

The only thing you can do with the deposit, during the tenant's entire tenancy, is put it in an escrowed bank account. This sounds intimidating if you have never done it before, but it is easy. All you have to do is open an account with your name followed by the word *escrow*, such as this:

Julie G. Wilson - Escrow

The day you get the deposit, place it in your escrowed account. There is nothing to keep you from withdrawing the money any time you want, because you are the owner of the account. The bank will not stop you. However, the escrowed account shows a judge, if needed, that you put the deposit money aside separately from the rent money. Escrowing the deposit costs you nothing and guarantees that the deposit will be there when the tenant moves out. It does not mean the tenants will receive the full amount, or any of it at all if they leave the home in disarray. Escrowing the deposit simply puts the tenant's money away until the legal time comes (after move-out) for you to decide how much is still the tenant's.

Since so few landlords escrow deposits, the judge has a surefire way of determining how accurate and lawful a landlord is. Although it takes much more to win an eviction lawsuit, proof of an escrowed deposit goes a long way to helping.

You can keep any interest earned from the escrowed deposit. Some landlords give this to the tenant as well, especially if the deposit is steep relative to that of competing homes. Of course, this interest is income and if you keep it, you must report it as such.

WRAP UP THE DETAILS

You also want to find out each person's name that will be on the lease. Explain that each person on the lease is responsible for the full rent, even if the other moves out. The more people on the lease, the safer you are. In addition, verify the number of adults and children who will be living in the home. Put this number into your lease in case you later find out the tenant has moved some relatives in and forgotten to tell you! In most cases, you would be wise to get a credit application for all the parties on the lease, including unmarried couples.

Do not turn over the key until you receive the first month's rent. This is critical: If you turn over the key earlier, your tenant can legally move in and take possession. Most landlords require a deposit to hold the property, then turn the key over on the date of the signing of the lease and the payment of the first month in full. This ensures that your tenants have a reason to take care of the home (you hold the deposit), and you have the first month's rent instead of an empty promise. Chapter 4, "Welcoming the New Tenant," explains the process of turning over the key. The deposit is enough to hold the home until the tenant meets you with the first month's rent. As an extra precaution, many landlords drive directly to the tenant's bank to cash the deposit check—if that first check bounces, you do not yet have a tenant.

Summary

Successful landlords show properties only once, understand how to use rental applications, and take the time to process applications in a legal and orderly fashion. At your open house, you are there simply to answer questions; you let the home show itself.

One of the easiest ways to avoid ever having a legal problem is to choose your tenants carefully and fairly. Check the local ordinances governing rental properties. Determine the legal minimum rental standards that an applicant must meet to rent your property. If you have more than one rental house, each one can have different rental standards depending on monthly rent, size, and layout.

Once you decide on the tenants, you must prepare them for their stay in your rental. Set up an initial meeting at the house and walk through all your rent procedures and expectations. The next chapter explains how to start off on the best foot with your new tenants.

CHAPTER FOUR

Welcoming the New Tenant

AFTER PREPARING YOUR rental beautifully for open house, you probably had a hard time choosing from the many well-qualified applicants. As you're beginning to see, landlording is rewarding and actually generates pride of ownership when you properly prepare the home, write an effective newspaper ad, and hold a productive open house.

By the time you sift through all the applicants and decide on the proper tenant, your work is almost done. After you let the tenant know of your decision to rent, you have one final but very important job to do—perform the new tenant interview.

Your tenants will be a most captive audience when you meet with them to hand over the house keys and to sign the lease. It is during this time that you want to set the ground rules for the tenants' stay. Sign an effective and binding lease, outline your rent expectations, describe your tolerance for noise and property damage (none), and explain your own maintenance policies to your new house guests.

This chapter focuses on the steps you must take to ensure as carefree a landlording career as possible. The tenants want the home, you selected the best candidates (you followed the tips in Chapter 3 to choose the right renter from among several applicants), the tenants paid the deposit — and you are almost ready to take a breather from your landlording responsibilities.

The New Tenant Interview

Select a time for the new tenant interview when both you and the new tenants have half an hour or so to discuss the details and sign the lease. The new tenant interview is vital. Without it, the marriage between you and your tenants will be more strained; with it, you start off together on the right foot. Nothing but time will guarantee wonderful tenants, but the time you spend on the initial interview will pay in dividends throughout their tenancy.

Treat the new tenant interview as a business meeting. Set priorities and goals, receive the first month's rent, sign the lease, and state your requirements clearly.

The new tenant interview gives you the chance to meet your tenants one-on-one. If a tenant has a family, attempt to get both husband and wife at the interview. Not only will two remember details better than one, but getting both signatures on the lease is better than getting only one. Of course, if you are renting to more than one unmarried party, you must meet with all of them since each must sign the lease.

Below is a list of items to cover in the new tenant interview, all of which we will discuss in this chapter:

- Welcome the tenants.
- Review the details of the lease.

- Sign the lease (two copies, one for you, one for the tenants).
- Accept the first month's rent.
- Turn over the keys.
- Discuss the rent collection policy.
- Review the walk-through checklist plus any other information you want to share with the tenants.
- Show the new tenants the location of smoke alarms, the fire extinguisher, the plunger, and the shutoffs for the electric and water.
- Walk through the house and around the outside with the tenants to acclimate them to the home.

This is the tenants' first and last chance to understand your requirements. They may not fully realize that fact unless you someday have to evict them. Hopefully, the eviction process and your tenants will never meet. Nevertheless, make sure every tenant on the lease understands what you expect. Be friendly but businesslike during the interview. This is the tenants' last chance to back out or to agree to *your* terms.

State your dos and don'ts in the tenant interview.

Suppose someday down the road, a neighbor calls to complain about loud parties, trash, property damage, excessive drinking, or even drug use on your property. Take care to check out the facts before you act harshly. If the neighbor's complaint is merited, your eviction procedures should be swift and firm. Chapter 7, "Handling Tenant Problems and Problem Tenants," explains the full process of eviction. Invariably, such problem tenants will ask for a second chance. But there is no room for a second chance with extreme behavior, especially if good relations with good neighbors are important to you, and they should be. Be sure that you can look tenants in the eye at such time and state that their second chance was during the new tenant interview when you told them you could not and would not tolerate this behavior.

During the interview, explain that the lease dictates your objections to certain behavior. Spell out that you will never tolerate loud parties, unapproved animals, any illegal activity, and all the other objections you may want to list. Tell the tenants that you like them and that their rental history was excellent, or you would not have rented to them. Stay friendly while listing your requirements. A good line to begin with is, "I don't necessarily think *you* will participate in such activities, but I tell these things to all my new tenants. I want to let you know what I'll do if you (fill in with your list of pet peeves) or if you miss your rent payment one time."

Introducing the dos and don'ts this way takes the personal aspect out of the discussion. You are telling tenants that you trust them fully. However, you do not really know them yet, and to be safe, you tell all your first-time tenants the things that you expect from them and the things that they should expect from you. This also gives you the chance to put your actions down on paper in the form of the lease.

Attempt to arrive early to the new tenant interview. This shows how serious you take your property management. Being "fashionably late" is rude to your new tenants and shows sloppiness on your part.

Two Common Lease Agreements

There are two common rental agreements. Most rentals require a six-month to one-year lease. The second most common rental is a month-to-month lease. If you and your tenant do not sign a lease agreement, a generic month-to-month lease is implied in most states. Your state's Landlord and Tenant Act (at the local library) will verify this.

A long-term lease protects the rent amount for tenants and implies longer occupancy for your property. A month-to-month lease is attractive to good tenants whose job or family requirements favor relocation soon.

There are advantages to each kind of lease. A long-term lease, whether it is for six months, one year, or longer, locks in the rent amount for the tenant. You will not be able to raise the rent during the lease period, unless of course the lease provides for such a contingency. Locking in the rent lets your tenant forecast costs over the coming months without fear of your raising rates. This is attractive to many renters, especially those in areas of high housing demand.

Some tenants prefer a month-to-month agreement. With this kind of lease, each month, either you, your tenant, or both have the right to change any terms of the lease; you can even write a brand-new lease with completely different requirements. However, if the other party does not agree to change the lease, the original agreement is considered complete and either party has the right to give thirty days' notice to the other.

Many landlords fear a month-to-month lease, but such leases are a little more effective in some areas, especially those parts of the country with low renter demand. A month-to-month lease gives tenants the opportunity to move any time, with no strings attached, with only thirty days' notice. Many tenants like this freedom. What they do not always realize is that without a longer term lease, you the landlord can adjust rent rates as high and as often as you think the market will bear.

A month-to-month lease generally demands higher rents than longer term leases for the same property.

Some wise landlords give their new tenants a choice between a month-to-month lease or one that is longer term. To the landlord, there is really little difference, except that the month-to-month lease can require slightly higher rent since it is short term. Just as a bank will pay higher rates for a long-term certificate of deposit (CD) than for regular savings, month-to-month landlords rightly need a slightly higher rent since the tenant can move with only a month's notice at any time. The risk to the landlord is greater with a month-to-month lease and a higher rent justifies the extra risk of more frequent move-outs.

Consider also the tenant who gets transferred or married or simply gets tired of your place and wants to move. Even a long-term lease will not keep such a tenant. Despite the lease, the tenant will move out and most courts will only award you damages for the time it took you to find a new tenant to replace the one who broke the lease. You will probably not go to small-claims court over the matter anyway; cut your losses and put your energies into the more productive task of finding another tenant.

Another reason that month-to-month leases are just as attractive to landlords as longer term leases is inertia. Most people dislike moving. Once tenants move in with a month-to-month lease, the odds are good that they will stay for many months and maybe years. They like the freedom of the month-to-month but dislike moving even more. You will have justified higher rents since your vacancy risk is slightly higher, but most of the time, month-to-month tenants will stay just as long as those with longer term leases.

Both types of leases are similar. They differ only in the payment amount and the termination of the lease. Both leases contain the same legal and landlord requirements.

THE CONTENTS OF THE LEASE

The lease you and your tenants sign will be a binding, legal agreement. Take it seriously and show the tenants that you do. You do not have to be a lawyer to write an applicable lease, and your tenant does not have to be a lawyer to understand it. You can modify the sample lease (presented a little later) to suit your own needs. A lease should simply answer the standard who-what-when-where-how questions:

Who are the tenants and the landlord?

What is being rented?

When will the tenant-landlord obligation begin and end?

Where will payments be made?

How are the landlord and tenants going to stay happy?

Give tenants plenty of time to read the lease, but only after you discuss its every detail with them.

You don't have to read the entire contract to your tenants, but describe the highlights, even if it means walking through the lease paragraph by paragraph. This isthe most important part of the new tenant interview. Everything you require should be in the lease. Although the lease binds both parties, current landlord and tenant laws favor tenants. It is not difficult for tenants to walk away from a lease, and most of the time, it will not be worth your time to go after them for the lost rent—lease or no lease.

A more detailed lease *generally* favors you over one that is less detailed. The more you and your tenants agree to in writing, the more bound the tenants are to you. Unless your lease contains unreasonable terms, tenants will be open and most agreeable to your requirements.

Not every clause in your lease has to be legally binding. Again, your lease must be reasonable, and it *is* a legal document. If you want the tenants to do anything, such as checking the fire extinguisher's gauge weekly, state that in the lease. But if a blazing fire demolishes the house, there is probably little you can do to hold your tenants responsible if they did *not* check the extinguisher. However, the requirement in the lease gets tenants' attention—most people take seriously the documents to which they put their name—and they will probably try to comply, thereby helping to maintain the safety of your property.

A SAMPLE LEASE

This section contains a sample lease agreement (see Figure 4-1). Modify the lease to suit your own needs. Over time, you will add and delete clauses, requirements, and details. Since tenants will sign the lease at the new tenant interview and you will go through it with them in detail, it's a good idea to include everything that you want the tenants to understand before they move in.

Notice that the sample lease includes the following:

- The property address, date of signing, and landlord and tenant names are clearly stated. This information is critical for the lease to stand up in court, if necessary.
- The language is clear but specific. None of that "party of the first part" or "the rentor or rentee" legalese. The

(continued on page 64)

Figure 4-1.   *A residence lease.*

Page 1 of 5

(initials) __*SS*__

__*DH*__

* Residence Lease *

This lease, made and entered into this __24th__ day of __March, 1993__,

by and between __Sam Garrett__, of __Miami,__

__Florida__, hereinafter called the "landlord," and

__Diana Haynes__, of __Miami__, __Florida__,
hereinafter called the "tenant."

The landlord owns the following described real estate and premises,

situated in __Miami__ County, __Florida__:

__1013 South Illinois, Miami, Florida 41127__

The landlord rents and leases to the tenant the above described premises

from the __first__ day of __April__, for __Six (6)__ months.

The tenant promises and agrees to pay the landlord as rental the total

sum of __Thirty-eight hundred dollars ($ 3800)__

payable as follows: __Three hundred fifty dollars__

__($ 350)__ for the security/cleaning deposit paid to landlord at the
execution of this contract. The entire security/cleaning deposit will be
refunded to the tenant within ten (10) days after tenant's normal lease
termination or move-out, whichever comes last, if the property is left in
move-in condition and will be escrowed in a safety bank account until such
time. The security/cleaning deposit's refundable amount will be prorated
accordingly if the property is left in less than acceptable condition. The

sum of __Five hundred seventy-five dollars ($ 575)__ is

already paid for the first full month's rent of occupancy (__April__). The

sum of __Five hundred seventy-five dollars ($ 575)__
will be payable on the first (1st) day of each and every month of the lease

Figure 4-1.   *(continued)*

Page 2 of 5

(initials) _S M_

_D H_

term (**Six (6)** full months) until this lease has expired to complete the full sum payable.

No part of said money shall be due and payable until the tenant has been placed in the actual possession of said premises with the keys needed to gain access. This has been done as of the date of this contract.

It is agreed that the tenant will keep and maintain all portions of the building let to him or her by the terms of this contract in as good a state of repair as the same are turned over to tenant. This means woodwork, walls, floors, ceilings, windows, screens, doors, carpet, shades, electric, grounds, plumbing, and outside storage, all of which may be inspected by the landlord on notice from the tenant of intent to vacate and in no event will this lease terminate unless the foregoing is acceptable to the landlord. Normal use without evident mars will not constitute violation.

The tenant agrees to be responsible to pay for the repair of any damage done to any of the buildings or grounds by any of tenant's family or guests. If the tenant notices any signs of property damage or signs of any negative physical attribute, including but not limited to water leaks, extreme floor or wall or ceiling cracks, insect infestation, appliance breakdown, or roof damage, the tenant will immediately notify landlord by phone or by written notice.

The tenant agrees to keep the property clean in and around the house and agrees to maintain proper sanitation of the area by preparing trash for pick-up by the regular trash service of the surrounding neighborhood, unless other arrangements have been made and agreed to in writing by the owner.

The tenant agrees to keep the lawn, landscaping, trees, and shrubberies neat, clean, mowed, trimmed, watered, and maintained as needed to ensure a healthy and visually appealing homestead, unless different arrangements have been agreed to in writing between landlord and tenant.

The tenant agrees to hold the landlord from any and all expense for lights, heat, water, or any other expense incident to the occupancy of said property, unless specifically agreed to in writing. The tenant agrees to keep these standard utilities connected and their corresponding bills paid

in a timely manner as required by the utility companies: _Electric,_

Gas, Water

Figure 4-1.   *(continued)*

(initials) _A H_
_D H_

If ANY utilities are not kept current, the tenant agrees to terminate this lease and give up the property's occupation at the landlord's discretion.

The tenant shall not engage in, or allow any other person, pet, or animal to engage in, any conduct that will disturb the quiet and peaceable enjoyment of the other tenants, neighbors, landlord, or use the property for any purpose whatsoever that violates the laws of the United States, the

State of _Florida_, or the City of _Miami_.

The tenant will keep no pets of any kind, inside or outside the property, without a separate and written consent of the landlord.

Time is the essence of this contract, and should the tenant default in the payment of any installment of the principal sum herein named, the total principal sum shall become immediately due and payable and the landlord shall be entitled to possession of the premises, at tenant's option

in accordance with the _Florida_ Landlord and Tenant Act, and the landlord shall have the right to store and/or dispose of such property in accordance with said Act, and thereafter the tenant shall be liable to the landlord for any amounts uncollected from such disposition, and the expenses therefor, including a reasonable attorney's fee.

The property herein leased will be used for residential purposes only and for no other object or purpose and this lease shall not be sublet without the written consent of the landlord.

In the event of assignment to creditors by the tenant, or the institution of bankruptcy proceedings against the tenant, such events shall cancel and hold for naught this lease, and all the rights thereunder, and possession of said property shall immediately, by such act or acts, pass to the landlord at landlord's option.

The tenant shall pay a late fee of _Fifteen dollars ($15)_ in

addition to each monthly payment that is paid after the _Fifth (5th)_ day of any month within the terms of this lease. Starting on the

Figure 4-1.   *(continued)*

(initials) _A̶G̶_

_DH_

Sixth (6ᵗʰ) day of the month, a late fee of _Ten Dollars_ ($10) per day will be added to the existing late fee due.

The tenant will waive tenant's rights under the _Florida_ Landlord and Tenant Act if the rent and all applicable late charges are not

paid in full by the _Tenth (10ᵗʰ)_ day of the month, immediately relinquishing possession of the property to the landlord at the landlord's request.

The tenant agrees to pay all rents and fees with a personal check, money order, cashier's check, or cash. If a personal check is ever not honored by the landlord's bank, for any reason whatsoever, the tenant agrees to pay a check charge of *Ten Dollars ($10)* then pay with cash until the expiration of this lease term.

The tenant shall check each and all smoke alarms weekly, replacing the battery as needed with an alkaline battery to ensure that adequate warning is provided. Also, the fire extinguisher's gauge will be checked monthly to make sure the extinguisher's gauge indicates a full charge of pressure.

The tenant agrees to keep the window screens on the windows at all times, paying a twenty-dollar ($20) service charge plus parts, if a screen is removed or damaged in any way, for its replacement.

The tenant will let no more than _Three (3)_ guest(s) stay overnight for a maximum period of seven (7) consecutive days in any two-month period without written consent from the landlord. This limitation

does not apply to immediate children of the tenant.

The tenant _will not_ keep any water-filled furniture at the property without the landlord's written consent.

The tenant agrees to keep no more than _two (2)_ vehicles, including but not limited to trucks, motorcycles, and cars, on the premises. These vehicles must be both operable and currently licensed. The tenant agrees not to repair any vehicles on the premises if the repairs will take more than 24 hours, without prior written consent from the landlord. Tenant agrees not to keep off-road vehicles, including

Figure 4-1.   *(continued)*

Page 5 of 5

(initials) _DH_
_DH_

but not limited to boats and trailers, without prior written consent from the landlord.

Landlord has obtained insurance to cover the landlord's interest and liability, but does *not* insure tenant's belongings or negligence.

The tenant will return any and all property-related keys upon lease termination, and give up Five Dollars ($5) per nonreturned key out of the security and cleaning deposit.

The tenant further agrees that after the expiration of the time given in this lease, the ___30th___ day of ___September, 1993___, without notice from the landlord, to give possession of property to landlord, and upon tenant's failure to do so shall become liable to the landlord for an additional one-month extension of this contract upon notice from the landlord.

Contact the landlord at ___913 East Oak Road,___ ___Miami, Florida   41156___

(phone: ___555 - 4321___).

IN WITNESS THEREOF, the parties hereto have hereunto set their hands the day and year first above written.

___Sam Garrett___   ___Diana Haynes___

(Landlord or Agent)   (Tenant(s))

tenant is called the "tenant" and the landlord is called the "landlord." (You might want to change the term *landlord* to *owner*.)

- Most standard lease agreements include the total amount of money the tenant must pay over the life of the lease. This includes deposit money that might be refunded to the tenant at the lease's termination. The money paid at the date of signing and the monthly rent amount are also clearly stated in the early paragraphs. Spell out all dollar amounts to deter fraudulent changing of numbers.

- The late payment penalties and the eviction rules upon nonpayment are specified.

- The lease is comprehensive, even down to the number of cars the tenants can have in the driveway.

- In the upper right-hand corner, both parties initial each page. The page number appears here, and the total number of pages is indicated as well.

- There is a location for the signatures of both landlord and tenant. If there is more than one tenant on the lease, each tenant should sign.

Depending on the layout of the home and the special needs of you and your tenants, you may have to greatly modify this sample lease. Most landlords opt to not use the preprinted lease agreements available at office supply houses, because they are too formal and rigid and contain too much convoluted language. By writing the lease yourself, you include the wording and requirements that suit your own situation.

A lawyer's eyes are probably better than yours!

To be safe, take your lease to an attorney for review before you offer it to the tenant. You will not necessarily have to get an attorney's opinion every time you make a change to the lease, but the first pass should definitely be looked at by a trained eye. After that, show it to a lawyer only when you make major changes to it. (Or have the attorney review your lease changes as often as makes you comfortable. Some people's tolerance for safety is greater than others. Keep your leases legal, but keep your costs down as well.)

If you run the lease by an attorney, be sure to inform the lawyer that you want a lease that is clear to the layperson but is still binding. Tell your lawyer that some clauses are for effect and that you realize they may not be legal requirements, but you feel better including them in your lease. For instance, if tenants go too long without paying the rent, the lease states that they waive their rights under the state's Landlord and Tenant Act. In reality, people cannot sign away legal rights. Even after signing that lease, they still have those rights according to the laws of the land. Nevertheless, it is not illegal for you to ask them to waive their rights upon nonpayment, and if the paragraph encourages them to pay on time, so much the better.

As with contracts, leases are just pieces of paper as long as both parties fulfill their promises to each other. Most of the time, your lease is a legal, binding obligation that you'll never look at again. However, when a problem tenant pops up, you will be glad you included every foreseeable clause in the lease. The more you both agree to, the stronger your position becomes if you have to go to court.

Feel free to mark out any wording not acceptable or that does not pertain to a certain tenant. Do so in ink by drawing a line through the clauses. Both you and the tenant should initial each marked-out passage in the margin next to the change.

If you opt for a month-to-month lease, only the financial conditions have to change. Instead of specifying the full multimonth rental terms, you only have to specify that the lease renews monthly. Still specify the deposit amount, late fees, and every other clause in the normal multimonth lease. For example, Figure 4-2 shows a month-to-month lease. Most of the clauses in both leases are identical except for the wording on rent payments and lease renewal.

Nothing beats a computer at changing and printing your leases.

Chapter 12, "Record Keeping and Computerizing Your Rental Properties," tells you how to use a computer, if you decide you need one. A computer is of greatest use to a landlord for lease writing and lease maintenance. A computerized word processor makes changes to the lease and printing it a breeze.

Retyping a lease from scratch every time you want to make a change takes too much time and is too prone to error. If you are the kind of person who will never use a computer, no matter how "easy" they've made them these days, consider hiring a friend or word processing service to keep your lease on their computer's file. When you need to change the lease, it can be done quickly and copies run off for you with a few keystrokes, saving you time and errors.

FILING THE LEASE

There is another little-known aid in the world of landlording. Your county clerk is the legal entity concerned about fair rental dwelling laws. In addition to being an upstanding citizen and landowner, everything you can do to show knowledge of the legal system will be in your favor if you ever have to go to court.

Filing a lease is easy. Just call your county courthouse and ask how much it costs to file a landlord-tenant lease agreement (the fee is nominal). While you have the

(continued on page 72)

Figure 4-2. *A month-to-month residence lease.*

Page 1 of 5

(initials) _SG_

_DH_

* Residence Month-to-Month Lease *

This month-to-month lease, made and entered into this __24th__ day of

__March, 1993__, by and between __Sam Garrett__, of

__Miami__, __Florida__, hereinafter called the "landlord," and

__Diana Haynes__, of __Miami__, __Florida__,
hereinafter called the "tenant."

The landlord owns the following described real estate and premises,

situated in __Miami__ County, __Florida__ :

__1013 South Illinois, Miami, Florida 41127__.

The landlord rents and leases to the tenant the above described

premises from the __first__ day of __April, 1993__, for each month
thereafter, until thirty (30) days' notice is properly served by either the
landlord or tenant, onto the other.

The tenant promises and agrees to pay the landlord payments as

follows: __Three hundred fifty ($350)__ for the
security/cleaning deposit paid to landlord at the execution of this contract.
The entire security/cleaning deposit will be refunded to the tenant within
ten (10) days after tenant's normal lease termination or move-out,
whichever comes last, if the property is left in move-in condition and will
be escrowed in a safety bank account until such time. The security/
cleaning deposit's refundable amount will be prorated accordingly if the
property is left in less than acceptable condition. The sum of

__Five hundred seventy-five dollars ($575)__ is already

paid for the first full month's rent of occupancy (__April__). The sum

of __Five hundred seventy five dollars ($575)__ will be
payable on the first (1st) day of each and every month after this lease
signing, until notice is given by either the landlord or tenant to terminate
this lease, by serving thirty (30) days' notice to the other.

Figure 4-2.   *(continued)*

Page 2 of 5

(initials) __*AY*__

__*DH*__

No part of said money shall be due and payable until the tenant has been placed in the actual possession of said premises with the keys needed to gain access. This has been done as of the date of this contract.

It is agreed that the tenant will keep and maintain all portions of the building let to him or her by the terms of this contract in as good a state of repair as the same are turned over to tenant. This means woodwork, walls, floors, ceilings, windows, screens, doors, carpet, shades, electric, grounds, plumbing, and outside storage, all of which may be inspected by the landlord on notice from the tenant of intent to vacate and in no event will this lease terminate unless the foregoing is acceptable to the landlord. Normal use without evident mars will not constitute violation.

The tenant agrees to be responsible to pay for the repair of any damage done to any of the buildings or grounds by any of tenant's family or guests. If the tenant notices any signs of property damage or signs of any negative physical attribute, including but not limited to water leaks, extreme floor or wall or ceiling cracks, insect infestation, appliance breakdown, or roof damage, the tenant will immediately notify landlord by phone or by written notice.

The tenant agrees to keep the property clean in and around the house and agrees to maintain proper sanitation of the area by preparing trash for pick-up by the regular trash service of the surrounding neighborhood, unless other arrangements have been made and agreed to in writing by the owner.

The tenant agrees to keep the lawn, landscaping, trees, and shrubberies neat, clean, mowed, trimmed, watered, and maintained as needed to ensure a healthy and visually appealing homestead, unless different arrangements have been agreed to in writing between landlord and tenant.

The tenant agrees to hold the landlord from any and all expense for lights, heat, water, or any other expense incident to the occupancy of said property, unless specifically agreed to in writing. The tenant agrees to keep these standard utilities connected and their corresponding bills paid

in a timely manner as required by the utility companies: __*Electric,*__

__*Gas, Water*__

Figure 4-2.   *(continued)*

Page 3 of 5

(initials) _DS_

_DH_

If ANY utilities are not kept current, the tenant agrees to terminate this lease and give up the property's occupation at the landlord's discretion.

The tenant shall not engage in, or allow any other person, pet, or animal to engage in, any conduct that will disturb the quiet and peaceable enjoyment of the other tenants, neighbors, landlord, or use the property for any purpose whatsoever that violates the laws of the United States, the

State of ___Florida___, or the City of ___Miami___.

The tenant will keep no pets of any kind, inside or outside the property, without a separate and written consent of the landlord.

Time is the essence of this contract, and should the tenant default in the payment of any installment sum herein named, the landlord shall be entitled to possession of the premises, at tenant's option in accordance

with the ___Florida___ Landlord and Tenant Act, and the landlord shall have the right to store and/or dispose of such property in accordance with said Act, and thereafter the tenant shall be liable to the landlord for any amounts uncollected from such disposition, and the expenses therefor, including a reasonable attorney's fee.

The property herein leased will be used for residential purposes only and for no other object or purpose and this lease shall not be sublet without the written consent of the landlord.

In the event of assignment to creditors by the tenant, or the institution of bankruptcy proceedings against the tenant, such events shall cancel and hold for naught this lease, and all the rights thereunder, and possession of said property shall immediately, by such act or acts, pass to the landlord at landlord's option.

The tenant shall pay a late fee of ___Fifteen dollars ($15)___ in addition to each monthly payment that is paid after the ___Fifth (5ᵗʰ)___ day of any month within the terms of this lease. Starting on the

Figure 4-2.   *(continued)*

Page 4 of 5

(initials) _A.H._

_D H_

___Sixth (6ᵗʰ)___ day of the month, a late fee of ___Ten dollars ($10)___ per day will be added to the existing late fee due.

The tenant will waive tenant's rights under the ___Florida___ Landlord and Tenant Act if the rent and all applicable late charges are not

paid in full by the ___Tenth (10ᵗʰ)___ day of the month, immediately relinquishing possession of the property to the landlord at the landlord's request.

The tenant agrees to pay all rents and fees with a personal check, money order, cashier's check, or cash. If a personal check is ever not honored by the landlord's bank, for any reason whatsoever, the tenant agrees to pay a check charge of *Ten Dollars ($10)* then pay with cash until the expiration of this lease term.

The tenant shall check each and all smoke alarms weekly, replacing the battery as needed with an alkaline battery to ensure that adequate warning is provided. Also, the fire extinguisher's gauge will be checked monthly to make sure the extinguisher's gauge indicates a full charge of pressure.

The tenant agrees to keep the window screens on the windows at all times, paying a twenty-dollar ($20) service charge plus parts, if a screen is removed or damaged in any way, for its replacement.

The tenant will let no more than ___three (3)___ guest(s) stay overnight for a maximum period of seven (7) consecutive days in any two-month period without written consent from the landlord. This limitation

___does not___ apply to immediate children of the tenant.

The tenant ___cannot___ keep any water-filled furniture at the property without the landlord's written consent.

The tenant agrees to keep no more than ___two (2)___ vehicles, including but not limited to trucks, motorcycles, and cars, on the premises. These vehicles must be both operable and currently licensed. The tenant agrees not to repair any vehicles on the premises if the repairs will take more than 24 hours, without prior written consent from the landlord. Tenant agrees not to keep off-road vehicles, including

Figure 4-2.   *(continued)*

Page 5 of 5

(initials) _A_ _H_

_D H_

but not limited to boats and trailers, without prior written consent from the landlord.

Landlord has obtained insurance to cover the landlord's interest and liability, but does *not* insure tenant's belongings or negligence.

The tenant will return any and all property-related keys upon lease termination, and give up Five Dollars ($5) per nonreturned key out of the security and cleaning deposit.

The tenant agrees that after the expiration of the time given in this lease, by thirty (30) days' proper service by either the landlord or tenantto the other, to give possession of property to landlord, and upon tenant's failure to do so shall become liable to the landlord for an additional one-month extension of this contract upon notice from the landlord. This month-to-month lease remains in effect each month, until a proper thirty (30) days' notice is given by either the landlord or tenant to the other.

Contact the landlord at _913 East Oak Road,_
Miami, Florida   41156
(phone: _555-4321_).

IN WITNESS THEREOF, the parties hereto have hereunto set their hands the day and year first above written.

Sam Garrett   _Diana Haynes_

_____   _____
(Landlord or Agent)   (Tenant(s))

court clerk on the phone, ask for the courthouse's full mailing address. Mail the lease with a check or money order for the filing fee, enclosed with a letter that says "Please file this landlord-tenant lease agreement." The court clerks will take care of the rest. Enclose a self-addressed, stamped envelope if you want a copy of the filing.

For extra precaution, file the lease at the local county courthouse.

Filing the lease gives you no more legal recourse than you already had. However, if you ever bring your tenant up before a judge, the more you did to prepare legally and the more you show that you take your job seriously, the more apt the judge will be to lean in your favor. It is no secret that the success of many legal proceedings is a direct result of preparation and commonsense tactics. Most of the time, a little bluffing is thrown in to win cases as well.

Bluffing does not imply that the courts are corrupt. Put yourself in the judge's shoes. Two people, with good backgrounds, come before you with two different stories. Many times, both parties honestly believe they are telling the truth. The more prepared party, and the one that followed legal proceedings to the letter, is the one the judge is most likely to view with favor. By filing the signed lease, you show that you regard it as a legal document, and your tenants have less chance of denying that they signed it. The date of the lease is also better determined, especially when you file the lease immediately after signing.

Collecting the First Month's Rent

After signing both copies of the lease, collect the check for the first month's rent. Don't make it a big issue—

just politely say, "Well, I need the first month's rent, and we're almost done here." Casually glance at the check as you put it into your wallet or purse to make sure the tenant filled in the proper amount, signed the check, and dated it correctly. Never accept a postdated check for the first month's rent. If you do, it could spell t-r-o-u-b-l-e for the rest of your tenant's stay.

Typically, the check will be the tenants' receipt. But have on hand a pack of blank receipts from your local office supply warehouse in case tenants request a receipt. Even if they paid by check, if they want a receipt, they deserve one, so be prepared.

Handling Keys

Now that you've received the rent, give the tenant the key to the home. If there are several different locks, provide at least one key for each. Always make sure you have copies of every key, since you sometimes will not get them back, despite the key-return clause in the lease. Of course, you can deduct missing keys from the deposit when the tenant moves out, but the cost of new keys is a minor consideration; you need a copy of each key in case you must enter the home for repair or in an emergency situation.

Pay a one-time fee to get every lock keyed to the same key.

Keying every lock to the same key (including any locks for an outside storage building or garage) will save you many hours over your landlording career. Keeping track of multiple keys is a nightmare, especially if you have more than one rental home. Your tenants will tire of so many keys, invariably losing one or more of them. After the tenant loses a key, guess who has to come up with an extra one? You, and it will be in the middle of the night, during a cold spell!

Explain your lost-key policy to tenants when you turn over the keys. Tell tenants that they will have to pay for extra keys. Inform them that you want all screens and doorjambs left intact, even when the tenants lock themselves out of the house. Tell them that although you do not want to come unlock their door every time they misplace a key, you also don't want them breaking a window or screen to get into the locked house.

Find a cafe nearby your own home where tenants can meet you to get a key if they lock themselves out. You can say that you'll meet them "halfway" to give them another key. They do not have to know that the cafe is closer to you than to them. After all, they're the ones who lost the key.

Whatever your lost-key policy is, tell them about it. The appropriate time to do this is when you give them the first key. Encourage them to make a copy in case they lose the original.

Describing Your Rent Collection Policy

The tenant interview is a good time to explain how you collect the monthly rent. Most landlords either personally collect the rent or ask tenants to mail the rent. There are drawbacks and advantages to each method.

If you collect the rent, you must make trips to the house each month and find a time when you and your tenants are available. If your schedules coincide or if your own home is close to the rental, this is no problem. However, you could be out of town on the due date or simply unavailable—and the first time you put something else ahead of your own rent collection, you wave a red flag to tenants indicating that there are other priorities besides rent.

Every time you see your tenants, you run the risk of them asking for something. They may want more storage shelves, more flowers in front, or a bedroom repainted (unneeded and never recommended if you properly maintain the properties between tenants; the only exception would be for long-term tenants). You must judge the validity of your tenants' requests — but be assured that they *will* ask for things when they see you. These will be minor requests that build up quickly the more you are there.

The advantage to collecting your own rent is that you get the rent on time and you see the property and tenants more often than you otherwise would. You can spot potential problems before they become big problems (such as excess trash and pets). Although you want to decrease the time you spend landlording, you don't want to become an absentee landlord. Be a part of your tenants' lives so they'll remember you when the rent comes due.

Self-addressed, stamped envelopes encourage prompt rent payments.

Because it's logistically difficult to collect the rent every month, more and more landlords ask tenants to mail it in. For years, utility companies have included self-addressed envelopes in their monthly bills. They want to make it as easy as possible for customers to get the payment to them on time. The customers have no problem with getting the address right and their bill paying is made easy.

Go one step further and supply *stamped,* self-addressed envelopes. Give tenants five or six of them at a time. This puts full responsibility on the tenants' shoulders to mail the rent. Although you are out six stamps, you help ensure timely payment, a trade-off well worth taking.

The only drawback to mailing rent is the check's-in-the-mail syndrome. When the rent is late, tenants can too easily say, "I mailed it, it must have gotten delayed. It should be there tomorrow since I mailed it last week." This is no excuse; on-time rent is the tenants' responsibility, not yours. No matter what the excuse is, explain that when the rent is due, it needs to be *in your hands*. Tell your tenants that you trust them, but you need the rent on the due date, regardless of delays in the U.S. mail. Tell tenants that if they're afraid of mail delays, they should mail you a postdated check a few days before the due date; you cannot deposit the check until the due date. Of course, the date on the check must be the due date and no later.

Most landlords offer a five-day grace period (there is one in the sample lease shown earlier). Five days is a large enough window of time to receive mail that was delayed a day or two at the post office. Again, the mail is not your problem. If tenants want to mail the rent to you, they must take steps to ensure the rent arrives on time, even if it means mailing early.

If you receive a late payment after the grace period that does not include the late fee, *immediately* send tenants a letter such as the one shown in Figure 4-3. This late payment reminder serves many purposes. It shows that you will never again tolerate a late payment without a late fee. It states your eviction policy for an extremely late payment. It shows you mean business. The next time you see your tenant, be as kind and courteous as you would be if you had not sent the letter. Don't mention it again, unless of course the late arrival occurs again. You will get your point across.

LATE PAYMENT POLICY

As you wrap up the tenant interview, explain what happens if the tenant pays late. Make sure there is no misunderstanding here. State your policy and ask if there are any questions. You are in business, and on-time rent is vital.

Figure 4-3. *A sample letter reminding a tenant of the late fee.*

October 9, 1993

Dear Diana:

Thank you for sending this month's rent. I appreciate the fact that you are a good tenant and that you take such responsible care of your home.

However, I want to remind you that I received this month's payment on the 6th of the month. I realize there are delays in the mail at times; I wish we could better control things such as that.

Nevertheless, your rent is due in my hands on the *first* (1st) and late after the *fifth* (5th). Because of mail delays, you might want to send it a few days early to ensure that I receive it before the late fee date.

I certainly understand that time slips by. Don't worry about the late fee this time. In the future, if you predict that the rent will arrive late, please include the late fee. (Our lease agreement states the terms of the late fee. After the fifth of the month, there is an automatic $15 late fee and an additional $5 a day after that. After the tenth, I have to start looking for another tenant.) I have to make a payment on the home, and my payment is dependent on your payment to me.

Again, this is just a reminder. I am very happy to have you as a tenant. I want to be the best landlord you ever have and that will be true only if I hold up my end of the bargain as well as I expect you to. Let me know if there is ever anything I can do.

Sincerely,

Sam Garrett
Sam Garrett

To be reasonable, offer a five-day grace period, as mentioned above. The rent is due on the first of each month and considered late after the fifth. If your tenants move into the home in the middle of the month, the rent can start on that day. If you have more than one rental property, a uniform due date makes things easy, so many landlords like to make the payment due on the first of each month. Prorate the rent for those tenants who move into your home midmonth so their next payment is due on the first.

If the grace period arrives but the rent hasn't, things should heat up fast. An automatic fifteen-dollar late fee on the sixth is being kind; starting on the eighth late day, the charge is five dollars a day for each day the rent is late. Do not make the late fee a percentage of the rent due but rather a fixed-fee structure such as this. If your late fee operates on a percentage of rent due and tenants are late with only half the rent, the late fee is less of an incentive to get the other half to you. Explain to new tenants that the full late fee goes into effect if *any* of the monthly rent is outstanding at the start of the late fee period.

Tell tenants that your late fee is extremely high for being just six days late, and the cost skyrockets after that for a few days before eviction. Let them know that you do not *want* them to have to pay the late fee. Let them know that the high fee is to encourage them to pay on time. Remind them that you can meet your payments if they meet theirs and that a happy landlord means a happy tenant.

Inform your new tenants that you start eviction proceedings if any part of the rent is outstanding after the tenth of the month (or ten days after whatever the original due date was). Be dead serious when you say this. But also assure your tenants that you trust them and just want to make sure they understand the rules of payment, since that is their number one priority, just as a roof over their heads is yours.

Some landlords prefer a more positive approach to a late fee. They like to offer an "early payment discount" if the rent is paid on or before the fifth of each month, instead of calling the higher charge a "late fee." Use whatever method you prefer. Paying after the fifth is bad, and negative connotations (calling the fee a "late fee") may be a more effective way to show tenants just how serious you are about paying on time.

The Walk-through Checklist

Give tenants a walk-through checklist (a sample appears in Figure 4-4) and allow them the first month to fill it out. The checklist is a form they fill out early in the lease period that states the outside and room-by-room condition of the home in the tenants' eyes. If you prepared the home properly, tenants will find little to comment on. Most of the time, they will return the list with everything checked off as being "in good shape and clean."

The walk-through checklist is really for your protection. When tenants move out and say, "I didn't make that hole in the wall, it was there already," you can show them the checklist, which proves the condition of the home at the time they moved in.

The faster the tenants fill out the form, the better. You can make it easy by letting them return it with the next month's rent. This gives them a chance to get moved in and to discover any little details that you forgot to handle when you prepared the home. The checklist also allows tenants to bring up safety hazards. Since they live in the home, not you, they have a better eye for potential dangers than you do. For example, a stairway without a railing may make it tough for elderly people to go up and down. You may not have thought of the railing yourself, but such an oversight could cause problems later. You should be glad when tenants spot a problem like this. Safety problems are best handled *before* they cause trouble (it is cheaper then also).

One Last Tour

Take your tenants around the inside and outside of the house one last time. Let them know that you want to make sure everything is clean and that the appliances work. This helps ensure honesty on their walk-through checklist because they know you saw the property *with*

Figure 4-4. *A walk-through checklist.*

---

* * * Please return with next rent payment * * *

Walk-through Checklist
(1013 S. Illinois)

Dear Diana:

Please take the time to go through each room to make sure everything works fine and is in good condition.

Outside of home:
_____Siding, shutters, windows, ground, screens, and storage building are in good shape and clean.

I feel I should bring the following to your attention:

_____

_____

Living room:
_____Carpet, walls, lights, outlets, ceilings, and miniblinds are in good shape and clean.

I feel I should bring the following to your attention:

_____

_____

Kitchen:
_____Shelves, sink, stove, floor, refrigerator, dishwasher, pipes, ceiling, and fan are all in good shape and clean.

I feel I should bring the following to your attention:

_____

_____

Bedrooms:
_____Carpet, walls, closets, miniblinds, ceilings, fans, and lights are all in good shape and clean.

I feel I should bring the following to your attention:

_____

_____

Figure 4-4.   *(continued)*

Bathrooms:
_____Floors, walls, toilets, sinks, tubs, and plumbing are all in good shape and clean.

I feel I should bring the following to your attention:

_____

_____

Other possible problems:

_____

_____

Tenant's signature   Date

them during the new tenant interview. Also make sure the tenants know where to locate the smoke alarms, the fire extinguisher, the breaker or fuse box, and the gas and water shutoff valves. Keep the fire extinguisher in the kitchen since that is where most fires begin. If you have an upstairs bathroom, show tenants where the plunger is (leave one for them in there). Urge them to use it whenever necessary to keep overflowing water from ruining their things and the downstairs of your rental house.

As you walk through the house, call it their "home" as often as possible. Home is what it will be to them, so acclimate them to that fact as soon as possible. A little public relations never hurts, and your attitude toward the tenants helps set the tone from that point on. Whether the home is a house, duplex, or apartment, it is home to the tenants.

Outside, show the tenants how to open the garage and gates. While outside, let them know how important it is that they get along with the neighbors. You might let them in on a little "secret"—the neighborhood is not a typical rental neighborhood (if it were, you probably would not have bought the house), and the people living around the rental own their own homes and take as much pride in them as you want your tenants to do. The tenants should watch their noise and respect their neighbors. You also want them to let you know if a neighbor starts causing problems as well (Chapter 6, "Neighborly Advice," discusses neighbor relations in more detail).

Let tenants know how you maintain the house and how you respond to repair problems. Assure them that you take care of emergencies quickly and other maintenance items within three days, five days, or whatever period of time is your honest assessment. Don't fib here; give yourself ample time. Your tenants will magically remember these words every time a problem occurs (even though the monthly rent sometimes slips their minds for a few days).

Tell tenants what you will *not* do as well. Most landlords do not mow the lawn, unless the property is a duplex, four-plex, small apartment complex, or condo. Tell your tenants that you will not always grant them everything they ask for, but if their request is reasonable or if it is an emergency, they can count on you to take care of it in a timely manner.

Being prepared for winter saves you and your tenants trouble.

Explain about winter conditions and how they can affect your property. If the home is raised above a crawl space, the pipes can easily freeze. Even homes on concrete slabs can have pipe-freezing damage in sinks and tubs that are next to outside walls. The best measure to ensure a smooth winter is to leave the cold water running slightly during freezing weather in all sinks and tubs placed against outside walls. The tenants can also help the situation by opening the cabinet doors under their sinks so the room's air can circulate around the pipes and warm them. Consider installing heat tape if you have severe winters (see Chapter 2 for details).

Let your tenants know how to take care of the garbage. The neighborhood may have curbside service or another type of pick-up. Tell tenants to leave no garbage around (inside or out) the home, garage, or storage building. Let tenants know the trash pick-up days for the area and how to prepare the trash for pick-up.

Saying "Good Luck!"

Your job is now done for a while, perhaps for many months. Your only responsibility is to deposit the checks each month — a job no one tires of. Leave your tenants the keys, a copy of the lease, a walk-through checklist, and your blessings. Tell them that they can rely on you to be a good landlord and that you know you can expect them to be good tenants.

Consider giving them one last piece of paper, a New Tenant Information sheet such as the one shown in Figure 4-5. This lists phone numbers for fire, police, and emergency assistance and gives the location of the closest post office, shopping center, and gas station. You should also include your name, phone number, and address. If there is a problem, you will want to hear about it earlier rather than later.

Discuss important details of the home, such as the location of the extinguisher, smoke alarms, and breaker or fuse box. This gives you one last opportunity to also leave tenants with a few of your requirements, such as how to handle plumbing and appliance problems. Tell them that you do not want them to call a plumber except in extreme cases when water damage is imminent. (Tenants might

Figure 4-5.   *A sheet of information for new tenants.*

New Tenant Information

Landlord: Sam Garrett, 913 East Oak Road, Miami, FL 41156, 555-4321
Fire: 911 or 555-3234   **Police or Ambulance:** 911 or 555-2982
Post Office: 13 Sycamore Drive, 2 blocks north of home
Closest Shopping Center: 843 Oak Street, 1 block east

Please check the smoke/fire alarms WEEKLY. There is a button to press that will test them. One alarm is located in the upstairs hall close to the ceiling; the other is downstairs to the right of the bathroom. For your safety, please use a replacement 9-volt alkaline battery if yours fails. The batteries are easy to replace if you stand on a ladder or stepstool.

Please do NOT store any items in the air conditioner and heater closet. The air is to circulate throughout the closet and it is so important that you will be damaging the unit and will be responsible for ALL REPAIRS including replacement of the entire unit if needed. I trust you and I only put it this bluntly to show you how important it is to me that you understand.

If you see a leak, turn off the shutoff valve to the tub, toilet, or faucet. Call me as soon as you get the water turned off.

Obviously, if you see a water leak, shut it off if you can and call me. IF it is an emergency and it is about to cause major water damage because of its size, call a plumber. For most "average" problems, I would like to be called first. In an *extreme emergency*, call Donald's Plumbing at 555-1109.

*** I have provided you with a plunger in the upstairs bathroom under the sink. It is VITAL that you help keep water off the floor in the upstairs bathroom, otherwise it will damage the ceiling and your furnishings downstairs if it comes through.

The electric breaker box to your home is located in the air conditioner and heater closet.

Please keep in mind that your lease extends to the outside storage building in back. Its floor, walls, and outside should be kept as clean and in as good condition as your house. If you leave oil drippings on the floor, I will have to keep part or all of the deposit. (Please use a pan if you store anything with an engine in there.)

Your fire extinguisher is under your kitchen sink. If you have to use it, pull the safety pin first. Check the gauge MONTHLY to make sure it

Figure 4-5. *(continued)*

---

is charged. If it is not charged, please let me know immediately. Usually, they hold their charge at least 2 years, so you should not have a problem often. *Please do NOT "test" it* by shooting it to try it out. This WILL discharge the unit and make it unusable.

Please treat this home with the care that it deserves. Please be aware of noise to your neighborhood. If your neighbors cause you trouble, please call me and I'll take care of it immediately. Conversely, they will call me if there is something you are doing that bothers them. I will let a house sit empty for several months rather than let someone move in who bothers the neighbors or who does damage to the rental property.

In return, I will be the nicest landlord you have EVER had, and if there is an emergency, I'll get it taken care of faster than you have ever seen. I care about you and want you to be as happy as possible.

---

think a Jacuzzi is necessary for occupancy if they had free rein with plumbing "repairs"!) List the plumber's emergency number but be sure to emphasize that you are to be called *first* if at all possible.

Inform tenants of the water shutoff valves under sinks and toilets. A water emergency is only an inconvenience if a shutoff valve is close by.

Unless tenants brought their furniture to the interview, you will probably leave the home together—you to relax and the tenant to begin the arduous job of moving. Sneak back, if you can, to leave a basket of fruit, or at least a thank-you note on the counter to welcome the new tenants when they walk into their home for the first time. This is another little expense that pays great dividends.

Summary

The new tenant interview is the most important step in hands-off property management. This chapter showed you the best way to present the lease, collect the first month's rent, turn over the keys, explain your late payment and eviction policies, and prepare the tenants for a happy and confident stay in their new home.

Congratulations! You can never guarantee tenant success one hundred percent, but you have taken all the steps necessary to select and prepare your tenants for occupancy in your prized rental home. Other landlords would like to be in your position. Despite all the work these first few chapters have required, you will now see how little you have to do to own rental property. Up to this point, the work has been an investment of your time. The dividends should now start rolling in—your tenants should be happy, and more important, *you* should be happy, especially with the extra time to pursue your other interests.

The next chapter deals with day-to-day tenant maintenance. Good tenants rarely bother you, especially after they get settled into their new home. Chapter 5, "Tenant Management," shows you how to perform top-notch duties as a landlord with a minimum of effort; you can be absent most of the time without being an absentee landlord.

CHAPTER FIVE

Tenant Management

THE DAY-TO-DAY MANAGEMENT of your property is not really that . . . now that you've prepared the rental and filled it with one or more good tenants, the real work is done. Most landlord-tenant problems occur because the landlord did not prepare the home properly or take the time to find good renters. With house payments staring them in the face each month, some landlords feel they must rent to the first tenants who want the home. But too many problems result from choosing tenants this way. You might get tenants who cannot, or will not, pay the rent. Even worse, you run the risk of getting tenants who will tear up the home.

Very few landlords want to be actively involved in their rentals more than they have to be. You would probably like to retire temporarily from your landlording duties once you've rented your property. The good news is that you can almost do that. One of the philosophies in this book is that you can be an absent landlord without being an absentee landlord; that is, you do not have to be in the middle of things all the time. You can put your rentals on autopilot and still be responsive to your tenants.

Be Selective But Responsive

Once your tenants move in, the most important thing you can do is show that you care. Never put the tenants second. If you make an appointment with them, keep it. If you promise to spray for bugs, do so.

You cannot respond favorably to every request. Do not feel obliged to do so. Better tenants will not bother you with petty requests. That is another reason that proper tenant selection is vital.

Write or phone your tenants. Only go in person when absolutely necessary.

When you need to contact your tenants, remember the U.S. mail. Even if the rental house is in your own neighborhood, a quick note usually is best to tell tenants what you want to say. For instance, If your tenants run out of rent payment envelopes, *send* more. Taking them in person wastes gas and puts you in the home, where you'll invariably be asked to repair, replace, or paint something. The postage you are out is made up in the time you save by not meeting with the tenants, and yet you have shown that you are thinking of them and that you are still part of their lives.

Suppose you are going out of town for a two-week vacation. Don't leave without letting your tenants know. Otherwise, a small problem could turn into a bigger one before you get back from your trip. Find someone who can manage the property for you and mail your tenants the name and number of that person. You can also call—but again, you want to minimize minor requests.

Only if the mail and the telephone are inappropriate for the message do you drive to the house. Making extra trips wastes time and money and usually is less productive than if you had written or called.

Writing and calling do not imply staying away from the home—quite the opposite. It's just that you want to avoid seeing your tenants too often. It is only human nature for tenants to ask for petty things when you are there in front of them. Maximize your efficiency and the pleasantness of your own life by eliminating unneeded trips to see renters.

Drive By Your Rental

Every time you are in the neighborhood, drive by your rental. Even though I encourage you to see your renters as little as possible once they move in, you still need to check on your property. By driving by, you can eliminate many problems before they balloon.

It is amazing how some landlords do not drive by, even when close, out of fear that the tenants will think they are being checked on. They *are* being checked on! This is your property! Make sure you do not constantly see unmowed grass, trash on the porch, and broken-down cars. The care your tenant takes now reflects on you in the future. You don't want the condition of the property to become bad enough for others to notice it. Rather, you want your neighbors to be glad you own it—and perhaps to call you when they have relatives who are looking for a rental.

Call your tenants when you see problems.

Feel free to stop and knock on the door if you see problems around the house when you drive by. However, even in this situation, there are advantages to telephoning instead. First of all, you may catch the tenants at a bad time if you drop in. It is always more proper to call first before visiting anybody. You, however, are the owner of the property, and a bad situation warrants an immediate knock on the door, rude or not. Usually, though, you will see nothing that warrants this.

When the circumstances allow, phoning distances you a little from the situation and from the tenant. Some tenants will feel less threatened if you call. Start the conversation on an up-note by asking if everything is okay and whether there is anything you can do for them. After the preliminaries, tell them you want to bring something to their attention. Small problems, such as an unmowed yard, stay small when you *remind* the tenant that the grass is getting long. At the same time that you remind them pleasantly of this, they are also getting the word that you drive by every so often.

Rent

RENT ADJUSTMENTS

When the lease expires, anything can happen. You can raise the rent, tell the tenants to leave, or renew the current lease as is. The sample multimonth lease shown in the last chapter automatically converts to a month-to-month lease at its expiration. If you prefer, you can change the closing clauses to state that another multi-month lease agreement must be executed and signed by both you and the tenant upon termination. With a month-to-month lease, you (or the tenant) can change the terms at the end of any month.

If your rent return is not adequate, you *must* increase it. There is very little you can do but that. Over time, insurance and repair costs rise and you can only survive your landlording experience if you cover costs with rental income. Few landlords can afford to, much less desire to, operate their rentals at a loss.

Give tenants time to adjust to a raise in rent.

Approach the unpleasant task of raising rents the same way you approach other rental tasks. Be businesslike but understanding of your tenants' viewpoint. Don't tell tenants that the rents will increase in five days. Give them several months at their current rate to get acclimated to the idea of paying more. (Of course, you cannot raise rates if a long-term lease is still in effect.) Raise the rents in small increments. Unlike the post office, which only raises rates every few years but does so in large percentages, be gentle with rent increases. A ten percent increase is about as much as most tenants will bear.

This means you must think seriously about the rates you charge before tenants ever move in. Try to predict the costs so that the rent is adequate and you can minimize rent increases. Tenants realize that rents are not guaranteed for their entire stay, but they would prefer to not have rents raised. They will be willing to pay more if the increase is not dramatic and if your attitude is understanding. Let them know that your costs have increased and that you have no choice but to raise their rent as well.

Tell tenants in person about a rent increase.

One of the few times a phone call or letter is inappropriate is when you raise the rent. Call first to arrange to meet the tenants at the rental home. When you arrive, sit down with them and explain that you have kept the rent as low as possible but that you must raise it to meet current costs. Explain that you want to give them a little time to adjust and that the new rent takes effect in a few months. If the lease has expired, let them know that you need to agree to a new lease but that you will go month to month for two or three months to give them a chance to adjust to the new rent. The odds are on your side; most people hate to move. Your tenants are likely to stay if the increase is reasonable, still competitive, and you have done your job as a caring landlord.

Be warned that you may lose tenants when you raise the rent. Like you, they have only so much coming in each month. If they feel they cannot meet the increase, be kind by giving them a good recommendation to their next land-lord (assuming they paid well and were good tenants). Being kind at this point encourages tenants to leave the home in good shape, and they may want you as their landlord again someday.

Instead of raising rents, you can try to lower costs — but this is rarely feasible. Once you've prepared and rented the home, there is very little you can do to lower your costs. Your loan is probably at a fixed rate, so that will not decrease. (You may want to consider refinancing the loan; Chapter 8, "Handling Money," discusses this.) If you are paying the utilities, you may have to be less generous and cut that out of your rental package.

Rents can *go down. You'll be a hero.*

Are you making *too much* money? Your answer is probably no and that is understandable. To determine whether you are competitive, you should research competing rentals to see how they compare with yours. Find homes that are as nice as your own and that reside in similar neighborhoods, then perform some rental comparisons. You will certainly lose tenants if you offer similar housing at a higher rent than others.

Attempt to beat your competition. You will have more tenants and fewer complaints. If you make a profit but your rents are higher than others, lower them. In the long run, the fewer move-outs you have will make up for the decrease.

LATE FEES OR EARLY PAYMENT DISCOUNTS

The leases shown in the last chapter included a late payment clause. The tenants' rent is due on the first of each month and is late after the fifth of each month. From there, a late fee escalates rapidly until the tenth, when you begin eviction proceedings. Unlike most of the advice in this book, paying rent late deserves no understanding, except in extreme circumstances. Only if the tenant has been the epitome of "good" by paying on time for many months should you consider letting that tenant think a late payment, with late fee or not, is okay.

To encourage on-time rent, some landlords call on-time payments "early" payments. Instead of a late fee, they allow for an early payment discount.

Use whichever one makes you feel most comfortable, but be aware that most tenants are confused by the idea of an early payment discount. After all, the rent is due or it isn't on a specified date. They realize that the early payment is really an incentive to pay on time. If that works, so much the better.

Early payment plans can be confusing.

To implement this approach, the early payment amount must really be enough to cover your expenses and make the return you require. In other words, the early payment must be high enough so that if your tenants always pay early, you will be comfortable with the income. The "regular" rent, which comes due after the early payment period, must be severe enough to inspire the tenant to pay on time. And to deal with tenants who pay very late, you still must incorporate a late fee structure into your payment plan. This simply increases the confusion without adding to the incentive. To eliminate unneeded confusion, reject the early discount approach; instead, charge a fair regular rent (a little lower than competing houses) and add a late fee for late payments.

RENT ODDS AND ENDS

Throughout your tenants' stay, they will have requests that you should consider, such as moving the rent due date. If tenants change jobs, their payroll date could change too; they may need a new rent due date. Don't be too strict on things such as this. The large apartment complexes are the ones that will not bend. You are smaller and have more flexibility than the big-time players.

Tenants pay for the extra due date.

Suppose a tenant tells you that he or she now gets paid on the fifteenth of each month instead of the first. The tenant will want the lease changed to reflect the new pay period. Changing the due date should pose no problem to you, but the tenant must realize that the first month of the change, the *tenant* must bear the extra fifteen days of rent. In other words, the tenant must pay forty-five days' rent on the first to catch up by the fifteenth of the following month. You should not be the one to wait the extra fifteen days for the rent. If you did, your tenant would constantly be behind by fifteen days.

Someday, you will invariably get a call from a tenant who cannot pay the full rent. Should you accept partial rent? The answer is a resounding *yes*, but the tenant has not helped his or her cause by paying only some of the rent. Until the entire rent is paid in full, consider the rent outstanding. The full late fee must apply or your tenant will not have as much incentive to pay you the rest of the rent. The rent should be the tenant's highest priority, just as the home is yours. In extreme cases, all legal eviction proceedings are warranted if your tenant is still past due by a single dollar.

You will have to be the judge of what to do in partial rent situations. Extremely good tenants have unexpected expenses they cannot control, just as bad ones do. If a family has prized your home for the three years they've lived there and can only pay one-half the rent some month, you may be prudent to take it and let them extend the deadline for the remaining past-due rent. Be firm about the next month, however. If you decide to let them pay late, inform them that the first day of next month you expect another rent amount in full.

Know Your Tenants

Keep a list by your telephone with all your tenants' names, phone numbers, full mailing addresses, places of work, and children's names and ages. Leave room for little notes about them. For instance, if you lease a home with a fenced backyard, jot down the name of the tenants' dog (if they have one). Then, whenever you speak to them, you can ask about their children and pets by name. Write down each tenant's monthly rent too, so you'll know that when they call.

The list will give your own family a better idea of whom they are talking with when they answer a phone call from your tenants. If you have more than one rental unit, the list becomes even more important.

This list is not just a ploy to make your tenants think your memory is better than it is. You *should* take an interest in your tenants. As long as you realize they are human beings and not just "the renters," they will view you as a real person too, instead of that *rich Mercedes-driving rich high-class rich mean rich landlord*, an image that the media (and other, less-intelligent landlords) promote.

Other Advice for Tenant Management

DON'T BE OSTENTATIOUS

After tons of success with landlording, you and your family will be swimming in money (we can dream, can't we?). Seriously, fortunes *can* be made in the rental property business, but they are only made over time and with lots of skill. If you do succeed beyond your wildest dreams, take care not to flaunt it.

Rarely do expensive clothes favorably impress your tenants when you drop by to change an air filter or to collect the rent.

When you see your tenants, consider their impression of you and don't try to be someone you are not. However, if you have a very nice car as well as a moderately nice car, consider driving the more modest one when you visit your tenants. Don't wear your best suit or dress. Again, you do not want to pretend to be very poor, but you do not want to put on airs either. Be humble with your tenants. Show them that you care about them, their needs, and their home.

LOWER YOUR TENANTS' UTILITY BILLS

There is a lot you can do to prepare the home for efficiency. Chapter 11 describes ways you can remodel your rental houses. It mentions several things you can do to lower utility costs for your tenants during remodeling. The more your tenants save, the more they have for the rent each month.

There are two easy, quick, and inexpensive things you can do to the rental's water heater to lower your tenants' costs right now. Although a water heater costs only a few dollars a month (a gas heater costs less to run than an electric one), over many months the bill adds up to a costly sum, which you can help shave. Whether gas or electric, check the temperature control on the water heater's tank. The control will be located toward the bottom and is usually red or blue. If it is as high as it goes (pointing to the side marked "Off"), turn it down a few degrees. Your tenants will probably be glad they no longer get scalded each morning when they first enter the shower. Most water heaters are turned too high for comfort and the extra degrees of heat gobble up money each month.

Your local hardware store can sell you an insulating blanket for the water heater. Buy one and wrap it around the heater, securing it with tape. The cost of the blanket is deductible to you as an expense, and the cents saved by the blanket pay for it within a few months. These cost savers help your pocketbook (when your home is between occupants) as well as your tenants'.

REMEMBER THE HOLIDAYS
AND SPECIAL EVENTS

If at all possible, budget enough of your rental income to offer a December discount. Figure 5-1 shows a holiday present that any renter would love to see. Most landlords rarely offer these kinds of extras, yet it is another way to show your tenants that you think of them.

Figure 5-1. *A holiday present for your tenants.*

Happy Holidays!

I wish you and your loved ones a happy holiday! I appreciate your renting from me. To help you celebrate the holidays, I wish to give you this $25 rent certificate. To use it, simply return it with your January rent and deduct $25 from your rent in January!

I hope you can use it, and I wish you well this coming year.

— $25 —

(Applicable for on-time rent only.)

Why is it that some landlords never think of their tenants during the holidays? Your tenants are your customers and you are in business. Businesses offer sales throughout the year to attract and keep good customers and so should you. If this holiday extra helps keep a good tenant, the discount is worth it. Your tenants are good people, but realistically, they have less to spend on holidays than you do. Your discount will help them enjoy that special time much better.

It is easier to keep good tenants than to find new ones.

There are landlords who like to give their renters a turkey, ham, or some other treat during the holidays. These are nice gifts too, and they add a more personal touch than a rent discount. Nevertheless, no matter how good the turkey is, the money will be more needed and therefore more appreciated. Either way, the thought is what counts. A nice turkey or ham is another way of saying thanks as well.

Be happy for tenants with a new baby. Send flowers loaded with baby's breath. In most cities a modest sum (deductible as a valid rental property expense) buys an attractive, delivered floral arrangement. While it's still fresh in your mind, add the baby's name to your records.

DON'T LET MAINTENANCE SLIP

Once your tenants move in, continue to maintain the rental. The tenants' faces will glow if you freshen up the outside paint job after they've lived in your rental for several years. Each spring, consider refreshing your rental in some way. You extend the life of the home, improve its drive-by appearance, decrease your fix-up costs, and most important, make your tenants glad they rent from you.

Pest Control

Some landlords consider their tenants to be pests, but this book is not for those types of landlords! The pests you need to control are those six- and eight-legged critters that every house gets at one time or another. If your tenants consistently dispose of the trash, wipe up after meals, and keep clutter to a minimum, bugs will find another place to thrive. Nevertheless, no matter how clean your tenants are, pests will enter the home.

You cannot police your tenants' every move and there is a fine line between ensuring tenant responsibility and overmonitoring their home. There will be occasions when you may catch tenants at a bad time—you'll ring the bell and find a mess in progress. Spills happen, clutter occurs, and trash piles up. Unless you see a continuing sanitation problem, keep quiet about minor problems such as these. Bugs will show up in a clean home as well as a dirty one. Accept pest control as a regular part of your landlord responsibilities.

Regular pest control is not too difficult to learn. The biggest expense is the sprayer, but it will cost less than one service call from an exterminator. You may cringe at the cost of the chemicals, but their price is misleading. Many pesticides must be greatly diluted, so that often you use only two to five tablespoons per gallon of water.

Even common household pesticides are *highly dangerous* if used improperly. Respect their use and storage instructions. Better yet, check out your local college to see whether it has an agriculture extension center that offers pest control advice.

Being your own pest controller doesn't always pay off.

Despite the danger, you can spray the home if you learn about the chemicals and how to apply them. The cost is low. When you call a pest control service, you pay for people's time, knowledge, and trucks more than for the chemicals. As with any do-it-yourself project though, you must realize that your own time carries a price too. Always consider the fact that every legitimate expense related to your property is tax deductible against the rental income. If you take the after-tax cost of a pest control service, you end up paying much less than at first glance. The advantages of spending your own time quickly lessen.

Use only licensed and bonded pest control services, because their exposure to liability is much lower than yours is if you spray the house yourself. If you spray improperly and make your tenants sick, you run a risk that you could have easily avoided by calling professionals. Learn before you spray or call an expert.

HOW OFTEN?

Weekly, monthly, yearly, how often should you spray? It depends, but if you have good tenants, you will have fewer pests. A pest control service will certainly be conservative in its recommendations, suggesting that you spray every one to three months. In many cases, this is probably more often than you need.

Some landlords, especially those with pride in their homes, rarely need pest control services. If you choose your tenants well, you can probably ignore pest control until your tenants see signs of activity and let you know about it. This would make many pest control services cringe, but the simple fact is that if you learn to inspect the home yourself for pests, and if you tell your tenants to let you know if they ever see problems, you can save money.

THE HARD ONES:
TERMITES AND ROACHES

Many homeowners fear the dreaded *termite*. They envision their home evaporating into dust in a matter of moments. In reality, termites damage houses very slowly. It takes time to notice visible termite damage and you can usually get rid of the bugs with few problems.

Because of the time needed to do damage, catching termite activity early is the key to minimizing its destruction. Most professional pest control services offer free termite inspections. The next time you call for a regular pest control, ask the technician to show you how to check for termite activity. If you routinely do business with the service, the technician will probably oblige.

The cautious can pay a pest control service to do an initial termite job. Because termites come into your home from the ground, the service will attempt to put a barrier between the ground and the home. Most pest control services guarantee that you'll never have termite activity after this initial service, if you pay them to inspect your house every year thereafter.

Less damaging, but more obscene, are roaches. Nothing bothers tenants more than these critters, and your tolerance for them should be equal to that of your tenants'. If your rental gets roaches, get rid of them immediately.

The sooner they are exterminated, the sooner your tenants will sleep. If a tenant's mess causes a roach problem more than once, get rid of the tenant as quickly as the roaches.

Roaches can be one of the hardest pests to control. Even termites have a more difficult time getting back into a house after an extermination job than do roaches. Although there are over two hundred kinds of roaches, fewer than ten nest naturally indoors. Most are brought in from the outside. Grocery sacks are notorious for hiding the creatures.

Exterminate every unit of a multiunit property.

If you have a duplex, four-plex, or apartment, spray *every* unit for roaches if you spray at all. Roaches are persistent and smart, although a professional can get rid of them if given the freedom. To eliminate them, each room in the entire building should be exterminated. Otherwise, the roaches will find the one room that was left alone. For bad infestations, empty all drawers, especially in the kitchen, before spraying.

Summary

Your day-to-day landlord activities do not have to be difficult. Most landlords put their properties on autopilot and spend time doing other things. Once you select good tenants, your job becomes a pleasure and you'll wonder why you do not have twice as many rental properties.

You can handle most of your duties with a letter or by phone. Don't drive to the tenants' house every time you want to tell them something. You'll waste time, money, and get a lot of trivial requests. Stay in the tenants' lives in other ways: Send them a card and discount coupon during the holidays. Lower their rent when you can. Freshen up their home each spring by caulking the doors and windows, by painting, and doing other similar chores.

If you prepared your rental properly, your routine fix-up chores will be minimal. The only recurring problem may be pest control, and even that is minimal if your tenants keep the home clean.

Now that you've made your tenants' happy as well as yourself, you must consider one other party: your neighbors. Most landlords do not concern themselves with the neighbors around their rentals. But those neighbors can be your best friends. The next chapter, "Neighborly Advice," describes the importance of these people.

CHAPTER SIX

Neighborly Advice

THE MOST OFTEN ignored aspect of landlording is the relationship between the surrounding neighbors, the tenants, and the landlord. The people who live around your rental house know the going-ons *much* better than you ever will. They see your property night and day. They see the good and the bad sides of your tenants.

As an efficient and effective landlord, you only see your tenants every so often. The more properties you have, the less time you should spend at each. There comes a point when you can spend only so much time with your rentals before the job takes over all your free time. This book emphasizes the streamlining of your property management. But if you succeed in streamlining, you will be around your property very seldom. If you trust your neighbors and approach them properly, they can be your round-the-clock house watchers and the best friends a landlord can have.

This short chapter offers neighborly advice. "Getting in good" with the neighbors pays dividends you can reap for the rest of your landlording career. The best rental homes are the ones *not* in typical rental neighborhoods. The best rental homes are found in neighborhoods with owner-occupied housing. The neighbors will naturally be suspicious of "that rental house" of yours until you knock on their door and greet them with your loving landlord attitude.

Get to Know the Neighbors

If you have yet to meet the neighbors on either side of and across the street from your rental home, *run*, don't walk, to their houses right now to do so. As soon as you close the deal on any future rental house you buy, be sure you've met the neighbors before lifting one paintbrush.

Neighbors are better assets than tenants.

The neighbors around your rental will be there much longer than any tenant you ever rent to. They have much more at stake in your tenants than you do. Their home life is directly affected by good or bad tenants. Their children play with your tenants' children. Their sleep is interrupted by your tenants' loud parties.

If you think about it, you will realize that the neighbors want good tenants in your home *more* than you do. If the neighbors like your tenants, you can bet that you will like them too. If the neighbors do not like the tenants, they probably have good reason. Their peaceful neighborhood may be jeopardized by your tenants. If so, those are tenants you do not want.

INTRODUCE YOURSELF

Before going to the neighbors, write down your name and phone number on a slip of paper, include your rental home's address, and write "owner" by it. You will give this paper to the neighbors once you introduce yourself to them.

When you first introduce yourself, greet the neighbors with a smile and tell them your name. Inform them that you are the owner of the house next door (or across the street). If you have yet to remodel the home, tell them of your plans to make the house something to be proud of. If you are a smart shopper, the rental house is probably a little shabby looking but is structurally sound. Anything you do to improve the appearance will make you a hero to the neighbors. The value of their homes is affected somewhat by the homes that surround theirs.

What they don't know is that you plan to make your home even better than theirs. They will be the ones playing catch up once they see the white shutters, fresh paint job, and flowers in front.

Get the neighbors' trust immediately.

Tell the neighbors the following: You value their neighborhood or you would not have bought the house. You will turn your house into something they will be proud to live near. You want them to enjoy having your tenants for long-term neighbors instead of wondering who the next occupants will be and what they will be like. Say these things sincerely; if you cannot, you will not have a success in this businss and you should try something else.

Hand the neighbors the slip of paper with your information written on it. Then drop the bombshell: Tell them that you want them to call you if they see *anything* about the house or tenants that they do not like. Tell them that if there are loud parties or too much trash or whatever you will handle the situation *immediately*. Let them know that your tenants will never know who told you about the problem. Reassure the neighbors that you mean to keep their privacy—and make sure that you honor your promise.

Tell the neighbors that if they ever see any illegal activity around your property or if something as simple as a party gets out of hand, they should call you immediately. If you do not answer the phone, they can call the police and you will take full responsibility for the phone call.

Implore them to help you keep good tenants in the home—tenants that they will be proud to have as neighbors. Believe it, this is not a job they will dislike; rather, they will be *very glad* they have a say in who moves in (or better yet, who stays). Tell them you will let the home sit empty for three months rather than let someone move in who might have a negative effect on the neighborhood.

Think how powerful this approach is! Can you imagine the respect the neighbors will feel for you? These people, who have a much larger stake in your rental house than you, now feel a part of it, and they know they can trust you. To them, the house is no longer a ghost property with people coming and going every six months but a home occupied by people whom you chose with care. It will be a home monitored by yourself, but more important, by your neighbors, for many years. Your neighbors will get along better with your tenants and you will have fewer problems down the road. If a tenant gets out of hand, you are going to know about it much faster from the neighbors than you would have otherwise.

INTRODUCE THE TENANTS

When you lease the home to new tenants, give your neighbors the tenants' names so they know who will be living there. Tell your tenants who the neighbors are as well. After learning each other's names, neighbors and tenants are more apt to say good morning and a neighborly relationship can begin between them.

Make your tenants and the neighbors feel special.

Better yet, after the initial tenant interview, take your tenants to all the neighbors and introduce them yourself. Be upbeat about the entire situation. After all, you may be building a relationship between the two that grows into a friendship that keeps the tenants renting your place longer than they would have otherwise. At the very worst, you will know about problems faster and will be able to solve them before they grow too big to handle.

Neighborhood Public Relations

Good relations with the neighbors is yet another way you separate yourself from the cliché of the uncaring landlord. Gaining the trust of the neighbors helps prove with deeds that you care about your rental home, its occupants, and the surrounding neighborhood.

The benefits you reap from good neighbor relations are plenty, but your aim should always be a peaceful and happy rental house. When your tenants and their neighbors are happy, you will be too.

Neighbors know who's best.

The neighbors are great resources for future tenants. If a neighbor recommends people to live in your home, you can bet they will be quality tenants. Still, perform the typical credit checks on them. But all you need for a character reference is the neighbor's recommendation.

Would neighbors be honest in their recommendation, or would they recommend someone just because they are friends? Think about it. Don't you have friends whom you love, and yet, you would *never* want to live next door to them? They might be loud, have too many children, have too many pets, be messy, or whatever. Most dren, have too many pets, be messy, or whatever. Most people would consider their own situation before recommending anyone, even a best friend, to live next door to them.

The next time your home becomes vacant, tell the neighbors that you would like their advice about renting it. They may suggest sprucing up the home in a way that had not occurred to you. Better yet, they might know someone who would make a good tenant and be an asset to the neighborhood. If you rent to whom they suggest, remember to send a thank-you card and a twenty-dollar gift. This acknowledgment goes a long way to ensuring future help as well.

ADVERTISE WITH THE NEIGHBORS IN MIND

When you place an ad for new tenants, consider advertising the neighborhood. If you were a tenant, consider your reactions to an ad headed with the following:

GOOD and QUIET Neighborhood!

All other ads will pale in comparison. Families and retired people will be drawn to such a heading.

Knowing the life-style of the elderly neighbor next to his property, one enterprising landlord used the following head:

Elderly Lady Prefers Same As Neighbor

The landlord got calls from more interested elderly tenants than from anyone else. Is this age discrimination?

The landlord knew, however, that many times older people make quieter and longer term tenants than college-age people. The pool of tenants to choose from was skewed toward the older group and the landlord found that the most qualified tenant happened to be the oldest applicant for the home. Several years later, the tenant was still happily living in the house.

TENANT-NEIGHBOR PROBLEMS

Although you've done everything you can to promote good relations between your tenants and the neighbors, you cannot control other people's lives. Personalities sometimes clash between the best of people. If you do your job—are a caring landlord to your tenants and a good neighbor to the rest—you will probably be called into the middle of the feud, and you must decide the next step.

Determine the difference between real problems and supposed ones.

The first part of this chapter emphasized how important your house's neighbors are. You saw how the neighbors' view of your tenants is usually better than your own. However, this does not necessarily extend to everday feuds between the two. If your neighbor calls you about a specific negative behavior, step in and handle the problem; evict the tenants if the problem is severe enough. However, if the neighbors call you to complain that the tenants do not get along with them (however they may phrase this), you will know the difference between a problem concerning rights and responsibilities, which may need your attention, and a problem of personality or difference of opinion, which usually you should not have to solve.

Here is where timing is needed on your part. You cannot, and should not, always jump into the middle of such a feud, at least at the beginning. You cannot police every little detail. Many neighborly feuds fizzle into quiet acquiescence after a while.

Summary

The importance of your rental home's neighbors cannot be overemphasized. The neighbors' view of your house and its tenants is probably more accurate than your own, since they see the home day in and day out.

Get to know as many neighbors around the home as possible. They can be a valuable resource for finding new tenants and policing current ones. You could very easily strike up a friendship between the tenants and the neighbors as well. If that happens, the tenants may stay in the home longer than they otherwise would.

CHAPTER SEVEN

Handling Tenant Problems and Problem Tenants

DESPITE THE FACT that this book stresses carefree tenant management, you *will* sometimes have problems with your tenants. You cannot manage rental properties for many years without running into a hassle now and then. If landlording were easy and took no time whatsoever, everybody would be doing it! Your aim should be trouble-free management, in as far as that is possible. From reading this book so far, you already know how to improve your odds at getting good tenants. You also know that honey catches more flies than vinegar does, and the more friendly, honest, and sincere you are to your tenants and would-be tenants, the more they will respect your wishes during their stay.

Not all problems are major. Actually, unless you get deadbeat tenants or tenants who are destructive to your property, most major problems can be avoided if you deal with them early. This might mean an amicable parting of the ways. It might even mean releasing tenants from their lease early, giving them a full refund of their deposit, or actually paying *them* to move somewhere else (it's been known to happen and, in some situations, may be cheaper than letting them stay). Despite good people and best intentions, personality clashes and difficulties can occur.

This chapter describes how to deal with tenant problems and problem tenants. When annoyances occur, you must decide if they are worth the tenants' stay or if they could turn into something more serious. Whether a discussion or eviction is warranted, you must be armed with a friendly but businesslike attitude and ready to take stern action.

Tenants do not always believe in a landlord's "conviction of eviction." Your tenants will probably assume you are not the type of landlord who would want to evict anyone. They are correct; you do not want to, but you know that you might have to at a moment's notice and you must be prepared.

Tenant Complaints

Tenants want to be happy, get value for their money, and have a safe place to live. They deserve all these things. Help them achieve this goal by treating them as you would want to be treated. Before reacting negatively to any tenant request, put yourself in the tenants' shoes. Remember that from where tenants sit, you are their caring landlord who showed them so much attention when they first looked at your house and when they moved in.

Assume that your tenants are honest until you have reason to believe otherwise.

Not all tenants are honest, but neither are all landlords. However, most tenants and landlords *are*. If a tenant calls to tell you about a problem with the house, assume it really is a problem and check it out. The worst disasters are not always true disasters. Each situation is different, but after a while, you will be able to read your tenants and their problems to know how to cope best.

Suppose a tenant calls in the middle of a blizzard to inform you the central heating unit stopped working and the family is freezing. The first thoughts that flash through your mind are the cost of a new unit, the cost of putting up the tenants in a hotel until the unit arrives, and the difficulty you will face trying to find the cheapest and best deal on a new unit. After your split-second of agony, calmly assure the tenant that you'll be right over to see what needs to be done. When you get there, you discover a tripped circuit breaker; in one minute, the heat is working again. Show the tenants how to correct this problem themselves for future reference and wish them a warm winter. (Warn them that if the breaker trips repeatedly, more than once or twice a week during heavy usage, to call you. Another problem probably exists in the circuit and you should have it checked out by a licensed electrician.)

Tenant Requests

Tenants must understand that you do not have to honor all requests. If they request something unreasonable, tell them so. Every time your tenants ask you for something, you must perform a quick cost-analysis to see whether you can afford to make the change (assuming it is not safety related, which is always warranted). The cost is more than just money: The tenants' happiness is also a worthy asset, depending on the quality of the tenants and how long they have rented from you.

If you feel that a tenant's request is unjustified, you might consider other alternatives before denying the request altogether. Suggest that you go halfway. If tenants want a garbage disposal, tell them that you will pay for half (including installation costs if you don't do it yourself), but the disposal must remain with the building when the tenant leaves.

Tenants have some obligations when making certain requests.

If the tenant balks at paying half and you balk at paying all, the stand-off might not be worth the hard feelings. An easy way of dealing with such a request is to tell the tenants that the house at this moment is the house they originally rented. If they want an extra such as a garbage disposal, they must pay more rent or help pay some of the disposal's cost to you. If the tenant does not like this, you can draw up an agreement stating that one of you will buy out the other's half upon the tenants' move-out. Approach such small "partnerships" with caution; buying the other's half is a lot of trouble, especially if you do not agree on a price at the beginning; and if the tenant removes the disposal, you must make sure no damage was done to the surrounding structure.

DON'T BE BLACKMAILED

Tenants cannot "hold out" rent just because you do not honor their requests. Just as you cannot shut off the utilities, remove important items from the house they rented (such as the front door), or sell their furniture if they do not pay, they cannot refuse to pay just because they don't like the way you handle things. (Of course, this excludes safety measures you've neglected and serious maintenance items you've left unfixed.)

If tenants hold out payment as ransom until you bow to their whim, deal a swift and *strong* hand with a notice of eviction (six o'clock in the morning is always a good time for a deputy to serve notice; it gets tenants' attention). Rent is not a tenant's bargaining tool. As long as a lease is in effect, even a month-to-month lease, the tenant cannot refuse to pay without being in default of the rent.

Suppose that when you rented to your tenants, you specified that they could not have a waterbed in the house. There are many reasons for not allowing them: They are heavy; before letting your tenants have them, you should make sure the second floor can hold the weight (a structural engineer can tell you). Another danger is leaks; a leak on the second floor causes havoc with your ceilings on the first floor. Since leaks are common, you should make the waterbed/no waterbed decision before leasing your property. Let's say you've decided not to allow waterbeds. You even included a clause in the tenants' lease that clearly states your waterbed policy. Nevertheless, your tenants call you one afternoon to tell you they just bought a king-size waterbed and traded in their old bed. They ask whether it's okay to put it in the bedroom directly over that new dining room ceiling you painted last week.

At this point, you will feel like the bad guy when you politely state your objection and remind the tenants of the no-waterbed policy in the lease. However, if you did not want a waterbed when you rented to the tenants, you certainly do not want one now. Here is what you can say:

> I enjoy having you as a tenant, and I hope the waterbed is not so important that it forces you to find another place to live. However, whether it is justified or not, I sleep better knowing that only regular and lighter beds are in the home. My insurance agent sleeps better also. Therefore, I hope there is another place you can store the bed while you stay in the home you rented from me.

Waterbeds are not the only change a tenant may want to make. Adding pets where none or only one was allowed is common. Most of the time, you find out about new pets only after the tenants have had them a while. The really bad thing about a pet is that once tenants have owned one for more than a week or two, the family will be very attached—probably more so than to your house. Such tenants will probably move quickly rather than give up the family pet. This is one of the problems with being a landlord; tenants never like you as much as their own dogs and cats.

A NOTE ABOUT UTILITIES

Once tenants, even those current with their rent, let a utility get shut off, you can bet that they will either move out or get behind on the rent almost immediately afterwards. There is rarely an exception to this rule. Some tenants have their phone taken out because they never use it enough to justify the expense. But that can be a hassle for you as the landlord since you cannot reach the tenant very easily. Feel justified in requiring that all utilities, including the phone, remain on and currently paid up. (The lease contracts from Chapter 4 contain utility bill clauses.)

Utility shutoffs indicate that rent shutoffs are imminent.

The utility clause in the lease gives you added protection to get the tenant out before the rent becomes invariably past due. You cannot evict tenants just because they do not pay their utilities, despite what the lease says, but the agreement does give you a little more control in a court battle if one ensues. It's just as good as gold if the house is in danger from freezing pipes because the tenant didn't keep the heat on.

The Offenders

Although you have done everything in your power to get good tenants, showing them that you care about them and the home they live in, some will still take advantage of your good nature and test your "conviction of eviction." There are not a lot of possibilities. Evictions usually occur because of lack of payment (including bouncing checks), disturbing noise from loud parties (the last chapter made it clear what to do if a trusted neighbor complains about parties), destruction of your property, major uncleanliness, and probably the worst of all, illegal activity on your property. You can handle many of the minor tenant problems without the strong arm of eviction.

An eviction bluff sometimes works but more often does not.

Sometimes, the bluff of an eviction is enough to take care of the problem. Nevertheless, do not use it too often. Either a tenant will call you on it and force you to take eviction steps, or the bluff becomes a cry wolf that falls on deaf ears.

If a tenant deserves an eviction threat, the tenant deserves an actual eviction. Except in individual circumstances, tenants were warned about eviction during the new tenant interview (an important process that was described in Chapter 4). When you lay down your rules at the beginning, in the new tenant interview, those rules are not to be broken. You are warning the tenant then about the peaceful neighborhood and how you want it kept that way.

TENANTS WITH RENT PROBLEMS

Sometimes tenants have requests that really test your mettle as a landlord. Say a new tenant calls you the second month of tenancy to say that an unexpected doctor's bill took this month's rent money. You have two options: Let the tenant pay later or evict the tenant.

The problem with the first option is you may be too trusting. The tenant's background checked out or you would not have rented the house. The tenant seemed then to be able to pay. The biggest problem with the news is its timing. Tenants who have paid on time for two years but need a break one month are much different from tenants who are only into their second month's rent. You thought you could relax for six months to a year but it looks as if you must go through the open-house, tenant-selection process all over again. With that staring at you, you will want to be lenient, but whether you should be is a judgment call that only you can make.

In such a situation, you would be more than justified to ask to see the doctor's bill. The tenant can cover the treatment information if the cause is private, but you have the right to know why your rent is being pushed to the end of the line. Remind the tenant that you trusted the tenant enough to rent to him or her originally. Also tell the tenant that you both just recently signed an important legal document, the lease, stating that the tenant would pay you in full every month. You do not take that type of thing lightly and neither should the tenant.

Think about changing the payment plan as a last resort.

Most landlords would evict these tenants, and such landlords would not be wrong in doing so. Heartless? Not at all. You can start your own charity if you like, but rental properties are not charities. Your first priority is to your own family. But what will the tenants do and where will they live? If they want to stay badly enough and their backgrounds checked out well when they applied, they can probably get the rent money from somewhere, either from other family members or from a bank.

Nobody wins with eviction. You lose tenants (albeit usually bad ones), your tenants lose a nice place to stay, the courts stay full, and the economy stays down. Before eviction, consider offering your tenants a *temporary* option. If they pay monthly, as most do, see whether they can pay weekly or every two weeks until they catch up with their other bills. You can draw up a very informal agreement stating that from a certain day of this month until a specific day in the future, the monthly payment section in the tenants' original lease agreement is overridden by a weekly payment. So many dollars are due and payable on a specific day of the week. Add a clause to state there is no late fee in this temporary lease amendment as no late payment will be accepted on your part. Figure 7-1 shows a sample lease-change agreement that you and your tenants can sign for this special case.

If possible, it's best to resolve problems without resorting to eviction.

Be sure such a lease-change agreement is very short term and ends on a specific date. It takes just as long to evict tenants who pay weekly as it does those who pay monthly, and giving tenants an easy payment plan makes you that much more vulnerable later. The easier you are, the more you can be taken advantage of, so be sure your leniency is limited.

Will this same scenario happen with your tenants? It may not, but there are a million other problems that occur without easy solutions. You must consider your peace, your income, and your property's well-being in order to reach the right decision for each situation.

Figure 7-1. *A sample lease-change agreement.*

---

* Temporary Lease-Change Agreement *

From June 1, 1993, until June 30, 1993, Sam Garrett, "Landlord," and Diana Haynes, "Tenant" (both signed below), agree to modify temporarily, within the date limits just described, their lease agreement.

The Tenant agrees to pay the full monthly required rent in four weekly installments of One Hundred Fifty Dollars ($150) due in the Landlord's possession on Friday of each week of the temporary time period.

There is no late statute or fee in this temporary lease amendment as no late payment will be accepted from the Tenant. If any installment is not paid on or before the due day of each week, the original lease agreement will take effect again, with the full past-due portion payable and due, and full eviction proceedings will begin.

Signed on May 29, 1993, by:

Sam Garrett   *Diana Haynes*
_____   _____
(Landlord)   (Tenant)

Whatever problems come up, attempt to resolve them without going through the legal hassles of eviction (a later section describes how to evict tenants). Use eviction only as a last resort. Alternative payment plans may help your tenants in a pinch and also keep them faithful to you for a long time. Don't feel like an ogre if you offer an alternative payment plan that adds up to a higher monthly rent than what your tenants normally pay. After all, it is the *tenants'* fault that the situation occurred, and dealing with it in this way requires more of *your* time and effort—for which you could justifiably require reimbursement.

GOOD TENANTS, BAD CIRCUMSTANCES

Tenants with good intentions and bad circumstances are the difficult ones to evict. Suppose tenants just cannot pay because of bad luck or the loss of a job. Perhaps they rented above their means but neither you nor they realized this early enough. You can evict them, but there is something that might work better and be quicker and easier for both of you — as long as the tenants are responsible in other ways (they are quiet and take care of your property).

Set up a meeting with the tenants at the home. When you get there, sit down with them and say:

> You have not been able to pay me for this month's rent. I think that you and I both know that this place is just a little more than you can afford at this time. I would be willing to let you out of your lease and give you your full deposit back, if you leave the home just as good as or better than you found it. Also, if you want to rent a place that is less expensive, something you know you could afford, I would be willing to tell your next landlord that you took care of my place, were good tenants, and that my price was just too high for your current needs and paying abilities.

After this conversation, the odds are good that your tenants will be *relieved* to hear this. First of all, they assumed when you made your appointment that you were going to read them a three-day notice for eviction or something equally bad. Instead, they heard an understanding landlord who wants to help them in an amicable way.

TENANTS WHO BREAK THE LAW

Some of the worst tenants break laws on your property. Drug offenses are common, but other illegal commercial activities could be going on at your property as well. But even these severe situations do not always require an eviction.

You must be careful how you handle your tenants' criminal activity. You cannot walk into their home while they're gone and snoop for evidence of crime. This is illegal, and in a free country, your tenants have a strong right to privacy. However, if you fix their water heater and smell marijuana or if a neighbor complains about comings and goings throughout the night, you have a responsibility as a citizen to do something about it. No matter how well these tenants pay, you do not want them in your rental and its neighborhood. You want to make it as difficult as possible for these people to continue their business; you do *not* want to provide them shelter.

If you have strong reason to believe illegal activity is taking place, call the police immediately. You can meet the police at the property or just report the incident and request that your name not be mentioned. If the police find a problem, you will not have to worry about eviction. Whether or not the tenants go to jail, their police record will be the only eviction defense you need. Again, a full legal eviction may not even be necessary. If the tenants are jailed, you have only to find designated family members who can take away the tenants' belongings.

Even if the tenants are not jailed, you can go to your property with an off-duty policeman to discuss the situation with the tenants. The cop can back up the fact that an illegal offense is enough to warrant and win an eviction. Tell the tenants (or any innocent family members left behind) that they must leave or you will have to evict them. Do not say you are sorry at any point in the conversation. This is one time when you are not bluffing about the eviction and when you should be forceful in every regard.

TENANTS WHO WRITE BAD CHECKS

Not as serious as drugs, but still a big negative, is a bad check. If tenants write you a bad check, make sure your bank ran it through twice. Most banks do this, but call your bank to verify the process used to return the check. A call to the tenants' bank will verify whether you can now cash their check.

Mistakes do happen. Ask tenants about a bad check before you take any steps.

Even the richest of the rich sometimes write bad checks. Math errors and spousal spending sometimes lead to bad checks. If you get a bad check, the tenants' bank has probably already mailed them a notice. However, they may not have received the notice yet. With luck, the tenants only made a mistake, and they have the cash to correct it. If tenants do write a bad check, for whatever reason, require cash or a money order or cashier's check from that point forward. This is a hassle for your tenants—but it is not your fault they wrote the bad check.

Some landlords go to the tenant's bank and ask how much they can cash the check for. Suppose your tenant wrote you a check for $500 but only has $350 in the account. You can request the $350 in payment of the check. Banks do not like to do this (it messes up their ledgers and their accountants do not like unbalanced transactions), but they will if you insist. The risk you run is timing. The longer you wait, the less the tenant may have in the account. But if you go too soon, you might beat a deposit that would have given you the full amount. When you request a lower withdrawal on a check, you usually give up your rights to the remaining balance, because the bank will consider the check paid in full.

Another relatively unknown tactic is called "holding for collection." This is rarely done, and many tellers may not even know it is possible, so ask a bank officer to help you. When you hold a check for collection, you put yourself next in line to the account's funds. Suppose your tenant writes a check to a doctor and deposits just enough money to cover the doctor's check but not yours as well. If your check is being held for collection, the bank waits until there is enough money in the account to cover the check, no matter what is next in line, and pays the money to you. Even if the tenant deposits a paycheck and wants cash back, your check will take precedence (that is, unless the teller is asleep). The drawback to collecting a check in this manner is that the bank will notify the tenant that the check is being held for collection. Evasive tenants will know not to make a deposit if they do not want you paid.

Some bad-check writing may be felonious.

If the tenant says, "The check should be good now, run it through and it should clear," be wary. You have every right in the world to expect and require cash or its equivalent when a tenant writes you a bad check. Inspect each bad check written to you. If the check says "insufficient funds," the tenant does not have enough money in the account to cover the check. If the check was written on a "closed account," you have a much more interesting situation on your hands. The tenant may now be a felon.

Writing a check on a closed account is a much more serious offense than writing a bad check from an active account. Call the tenant's bank to find out the date the account was closed. If that date falls before the check's, the tenant probably knowingly wrote a check on a closed account. But again, a simple phone call is first in order. Maybe the tenant's spouse closed the account because he or she found a better interest rate elsewhere and the tenant failed to remember this when your check was written. This is a long shot but worth checking out.

If the closed account is not easily explained and corrected with cash, your town's local district attorney may be interested in the problem of checks written knowingly on a closed account. Even if the D.A. does not seem interested, report it. A hot check deserves immediate cash payment, although an eviction is probably more appropriate in most cases. Nothing should be more important on your list of tenants' priorities than paying you in full and on time. If something else gets in the way of that, eviction will at least ensure that they don't do it to you twice.

Getting Rid of Bad Tenants

If your tenants deserve eviction, you must act swiftly. Illegal activities and lack of payment deserve nothing less in most cases. Of course, each situation requires your thought and not every situation warrants eviction. Try eviction last; attempt to work with your tenants, especially ones that have been good up until the problem began.

Your state's Landlord and Tenant Act (available at your county library) describes your rights to evict as a landlord. The sad news is that most landlords rarely read this important governing document. The good news is that most tenants fail to read it also. The odds are on your side if you follow the act's rules regarding landlording and eviction allowances.

Most counties' small-claims courts handle evictions. Normally, you do not need a lawyer, especially if you do your homework. Take with you to court all records (including the details of payment, or lack of payment) that pertain to the current tenants' occupancy. Show proof that you properly escrowed the deposit. If you filed the lease at the courthouse when the tenants moved in, bring a certified copy of the filing to the initial hearing. If you did your part (especially escrowing the deposit, which most landlords fail to do), there is little chance the tenants will win.

Show up at the eviction hearing and hope the tenant does not.

When tenants are sued in court (and eviction is a form of suing), they must show up to the hearing or automatically receive a guilty verdict. Tenants do not always show up for eviction hearings. Most of them know they will lose, especially if you have been a first-class landlord in every way. What tenants may not realize is that today's court system is a system of bargains. You may want your $750 in unpaid rent plus court costs, but tenants might be able to get the judge to lower the judgment amount. Such judgments are not always fair (many courts are too liberal in most landlords' eyes), but tenants give up *all* bargaining power by not showing up. No defense means guilt by default.

Just because a judge rules in your favor, awarding bargained or full damages, it does not mean you will get your money. But that is *not* your primary goal: Throughout the entire eviction, keep focused on getting the bad tenants out of your rental and good ones into it. So be aware that, even if the judge rules in your favor, not all tenants will pay you. You can garnish their wages for past-due rent, but you will have to pay added court costs—and you still may not get the rent if a tenant later quits or loses his or her job.

If all else fails, you can request a body attachment; a deputy will pick up the tenant and jail him or her. Again, the cost of this lies with you, but the tenant will not be doing the same thing to another landlord down the road. Cost, trouble, guilt, and even fear keep many landlords from going this far. Your role is not District Attorney but Likeable Landlord. Make sure that getting the old tenant out and a new one in is your primary concern.

THE STEPS TO EVICTION

To make an eviction, you must follow several steps. Check with your state's most recent Landlord and Tenant Act (at your local county library) to make sure what these steps are for your state. Eviction means a court appearance and to get someone in court means that you must inform that person of your intent to sue (called "giving proper service").

You must do the following to evict a tenant:

1. File an action for eviction with your county's local small-claims court. The clerk will set a date for your court appearance, of which the tenant must be told. The clerk will ask how you want the notice served to the defendant (you are the *plaintiff* and the tenant is the *defendant*) (read step 2 below to learn about the serving of the notice). You and the clerk must ensure that proper time is given between the serving of the eviction paper and the court appearance.

Rarely does it pay to hire an attorney for eviction proceedings in small-claims court.

Although an attorney's recommendation is always safer than not having one (sometimes too safe), you have little need for an attorney in an eviction proceeding. Small-claims court costs are minimal, and your damages rarely justify the expense of an attorney. One of the only exceptions is if your tenant has done severe damage to your property and you are suing for an extremely large amount. If the suit is too large (the amount varies state by state), the small-claims court will refuse to hear the case and you will have to move it (with the help of an attorney) to a higher court.

The eviction steps described in these pages are merely guidelines. The actual process varies from state to state. The county court clerk will help you with the details and verify that your eviction notice is proper for your state.

2. You must serve, or have served, a proper eviction notice informing tenants of the court appearance and the reason for the suit. State the tenants' names (as they appear on the lease; be sure to include *every* name on the lease if you rent to more than one person), the property's address, the total amount of rent and late fees due as of the date of the serving, the reason for eviction (a one-sentence general description is better than details), and the date of the court appearance. Sign the notice. Figure 7-2 shows a sample eviction notice that you can modify to meet your own needs. It is most important that you properly serve the tenants. You can call your local sheriff's office for a brochure of proper serving requirements.

Better than serving notice yourself, although a little more expensive, is hiring it out. The sheriff's office will serve your notice, usually within three days, for a moderate fee. The sheriff's office will ensure that the notice is properly served. In addition, a sheriff's car and uniform is a little more intimidating than a landlord's suit. The drawback to using the sheriff is that there may be a backlog of notices that must be served before yours. When you evict a tenant, you want the wheels of justice to turn as quickly as possible. Three days is a long time before the tenant gets the notice; from there, your county's ordinances will dictate how many days the tenant gets before going to court.

More timely, and a little more personal, is hiring an off-duty police officer to serve the notice. Find an officer who is interested in serving an eviction notice during off-duty time for a fair fee. The officer will appear at the property to serve notice, at a time agreed on by both of you. The officer will be familiar with proper serving requirements and will get the notice served quicker than the sheriff's office usually can. He or she will also appreciate the extra income. Pay the officer (they usually prefer cash) the same amount as the sheriff's office requires. The money will be more appreciated and will not get eaten up by a lot of red tape.

Figure 7-2.   *A sample eviction notice.*

---

* Notice of Eviction Proceedings *

Sam Garrett, undersigned "Landlord," immediately requests the vacancy of Diana Haynes, the "Tenant," currently in possession of the property located at:

1013 S. Illinois, Miami, Florida 41127

The Tenant is hereby requested to appear at the eviction and rent collection hearing at 9:30 A.M., Monday, May 18, 1993, at the Miami County Courthouse.

This eviction proceeding was initiated by the Landlord to collect all past-due rents and fees and to require the immediate vacancy of the said property by the Tenant. The past-due rent and fees sum to Eight Hundred Seventy Dollars ($870).

This notice is signed on the following date by the Landlord:

Sam Garrett _____ Date: 5-7-93
                                         (Landlord)

On 5/7/93, OFFICER #761 *Jayne Underwood*
properly served this eviction notice.

Whether the sheriff's office or a police officer serves the notice, get the server to sign a statement at the bottom of the notice (and on your copy) that says something similar to "Officer Jayne Underwood properly served this eviction notice on this 8th day of November, 1993." You will then have a record that the server properly served the notice, and it will be difficult for the tenant to maintain that he or she never received it.

3. Appear in court. In small-claims court, you'll be representing yourself, so take all your records, including the bank account statement showing that you properly escrowed the tenants' security and cleaning deposit. State the facts but do not speak until the judge asks you to. You

are dealing all the cards in this case so don't lose your cool. The tenants are the ones who must defend your allegations. Even though defendants are innocent until proved guilty, eviction laws are clear and you are prepared to justify your side of the case.

4. Upon awarding you damages, the court will require the tenants to make all payments, including past-due rents and late fees, to you. Inform the judge of the original deposit's amount and ask if you can apply it to the judgment. Although the deposit is not meant to be used for past-due rent, the judge will almost invariably rule that you can use it in this case.

If the judge lets you use the deposit for part of the past-due rent, you may still have a problem. If the tenants are still in residence, you haven't been able to inspect the home's move-out condition, so you don't know how much of the deposit will be left. Ask the judge what you can do in this case. He or she will probably allow you to use your own judgment when the time comes and to keep however much of the deposit is left, once you clean up and make necessary repairs.

If the tenants do not have the money, the judge will dictate a payment schedule or ask you and your tenants to determine one. The judge has the right to delve into the tenants' financial status to determine exactly how long they have to pay you full restitution.

You cannot get blood from a turnip nor money from a tenant who simply will not pay.

The judge will also specify the date that the tenants must vacate the premises if they have not already done so (most tenants will already be out by this time). Giving them three to five days to move is fair. If the judge is a little more lenient with tenants and allows them one or two weeks, *politely* state that you need to rent the property as soon as possible. Ask if there is any way the judge can shorten the tenants' occupancy. Rarely will a judge change an initial declaration, but you have a chance if you are humble and polite.

5. If the judge has set up a payment schedule, you must wait for the tenant to pay you. While waiting, begin the process of getting good tenants into the home. An empty house invites trouble (some insurance policies require your rental property to be rented before the policy is valid), so do not let the negative of the eviction outweigh your positive attitude toward the house. Again, if landlording were extremely easy, everybody would have rental properties and the competition would be fierce.

If tenants fail to pay you according to the schedule agreed to in or dictated by the court, you can garnish their wages. But garnishment requires another court appearance by you, including more costs. At this point, you may have to drop the eviction case if the additional costs do not seem to justify the possible income. Getting the tenants out of the house is more important than squeezing past-due rent from tenants who refuse to pay.

If you decide to continue with the garnishment, you must be able to find where the tenant works. Not all employers are supportive of wage garnishments, but they will respond if the court requires it. If the tenant does not have a job, or if you cannot find where the tenant works, you can get a *body attachment*, which allows the sheriff to arrest and jail the tenant until the money is paid to you.

Of course, jailed tenants cannot get your money to you if they do not have it, so make the body attachment procedure your last resort. Nevertheless, if a tenant is simply not going to pay you, do not feel guilty about the body attachment; the tenant would probably stiff the next landlord, and this country did not become a world power by providing rent-free housing.

If the tenants have not vacated the premises by the court's determined date, a sheriff will help move them out for you. This can get messy, so ask the sheriff's office about its procedures. It is easier to evict the tenant than to recover past-due rents, and more important to you anyway.

HOW MUCH OF THE DEPOSIT?

Once tenants vacate the premises, you must determine the amount of the damages to be taken out of the security/cleaning deposit. Remember that the escrowed deposit is not yours but the tenants', unless they leave the house dirty or damaged. Once the tenants are out, compare their walk-through checklist with the present condition of the home (the checklist, which describes the condition of the home when the tenants moved in, was discussed in Chapter 4).

If you must use some or all of the deposit for cleaning and damages, detail exactly how much you will deduct and keep all receipts as proof. Do not list "$25 cleaning costs" because this does not provide enough justification. Instead, be very specific. Remember, you cannot charge for your own labor; but you can hire others to clean the house and deduct their costs, if reasonable, from the deposit.

Some states require you to send the remaining deposit, if any, plus a detailed schedule of deposit deductions, to the tenants by registered mail. Your state's Landlord and Tenant Act describes how to return the deposit and the description of charges against the deposit. Of course, if the judge said during the eviction hearing that you can use whatever is left of the deposit for past-due rents and fees, list the remaining amount you used to offset these rents and fees with the other charges against the deposit. Mail the tenant this description if the state requires you to do so.

Summary

There are many ways to get rid of bad tenants, but the end result is the only thing that matters: getting them out *as soon as possible*. You may have heard that it is difficult to evict certain people, but you won't have a problem if you follow proper small-claims proceedings and keep proper records. Sometimes, the eviction notice is the only thing needed to get rid of tenants (although getting past-due rents may be tougher).

Eviction should be swift, firm, and businesslike. Eviction is tough but having bad tenants is much worse than having no tenants. The courts will eventually attempt to equalize your situation if you have the patience. Even if you do not get your past-due rent, and even if your home sits empty while you look for good tenants, you are better off without bad tenants than with them.

After an eviction, can you find good tenants? Of course you can! After several months with good tenants, you'll forget you ever saw a bad one. There are millions of people out there who want to rent from a good landlord like you. And with the precautions described in the earlier chapters, you will be able to find the right tenants for your rental.

CHAPTER EIGHT

Handling Money

YOU MAY HAVE originally gotten into the rental property business by accident, which happens to many people. You may have inherited an extra house or gotten stuck with one you can't sell because of a housing slump. If you are an "accidental" landlord—thrown into the job without asking—this book has so far given you advice on making your day-to-day management easier. But you also need advice on how to handle your rental property finances. (If you have yet to acquire rental property but are interested in doing so, read the next chapter, "Thinking About Landlording?" It will give you an idea of some of the things you can expect as a new rental property owner.)

By implementing the guidelines in this book (and some shortcuts of your own) you will rent your properties to good people who stay a long time. This not only translates into less hassle for you but more money as well. Less maintenance, less advertising, and fewer turnovers all combine to release you from the financial burdens that problem tenants can cause. By reading the early chapters of this book, you now know that a little money and effort up front make more money in the long run. Landlords who are chintzy on spending for upkeep and tenant recruiting are out more dollars in the long run and have much worse tenants.

Once you begin to keep more of your rent money, you must find ways to manage it and increase it. This chapter discusses the important aspects of rental property finances that you should consider: profits, insurance, taxes, expenses, mortgages, appreciation, and depreciation.

Your Profit Picture

The rental property you own *must* make money. Because of taxes, insurance, vacancies,and repairs, you can't expect your property to make money *every* month. But over several months, it should produce more money than it consumes. If it doesn't, you're in trouble—and unfortunately, there are very few ways to decrease costs in the hope of improving your profit picture. Although this chapter discusses one common method of doing so (refinancing a high-interest mortgage), if your expenses are as low as possible and your rents are as high as the market will bear, yet your property still loses money, you have only one alternative: Sell it.

WHEN SELLING IS NOT EASY

Even in depressed times, rental properties can offer very attractive returns for their landlords. Whether savings interest rates are high or low, the prudent landlord will almost always beat the interest rates of banks and CDs (certificates of deposits), often by a large amount. However, if you cannot make money with your property, you probably should sell it. If selling is difficult, find out whether your loan is *assumable*. If buyers can assume your loan, they'll find the purchase of your property more attractive.

If the interest rate on your mortgage is lower than that of current mortgage rates, an assumable loan offers buyers a better rate than they can get elsewhere. However, not every seller would feel comfortable letting a second party assume the loan. If the buyer defaults on the loan, the bank may be able to come back to you, perhaps years later, for the balance. By then, the "buyer" would have paid the loan down some, so this is not always a negative for you.

Some lenders will remove your name from an assumed mortgage after a period of time.

Before letting someone assume your loan, ask your mortgage lender for its policy on removing your name from the loan after the assumer maintains a good payment record for a while. Most lenders will let you off the hook in a year or two. But lenders do not have to do this. The more people responsible for a loan, the better are the lender's chances of collecting the loan.

Not all loans can be assumed. Also, if your loan's interest rate is not competitive with today's rates, an assumable loan would only be attractive to buyers with poor credit ratings; these people cannot get a loan of their own so they look for a nonqualifying loan to assume. These people are certainly not all crooked. Some of them just want a chance to improve their credit history, and they want to own their own home. To protect yourself, however, understand the buyers' financial situation before letting them assume your loan.

If you can find no buyers interested in assuming your loan, you have only one solution: Lower the selling price until the home sells. Only you can determine how low to go before you lose even more money on the sale than you would from the rent. A banker can help you with the computation (called "time value of money"). If you are losing one hundred dollars a month after all expenses, it wouldn't take you too long to make up a one-thousand-dollar reduction in price in order to sell the house quickly.

SELL DESPITE TAX PROFITS

Probably the last advice you thought you would get in a landlording book is to sell the house. Nevertheless, prudent landlords know when to cut their losses. If you find that you are losing a hundred dollars each month, you know you could invest that money much better elsewhere.

Watch your losses. Over time, a small loss becomes a large one.

Many people own a rental house that loses only ten to fifty dollars a month. They feel justified in keeping it because they are out so very little. However, as your banker will tell you, twenty-five dollars a month over several years adds up to a tremendous sum. Compare a landlord who loses twenty-five dollars a month with one who profits by that amount each month. How many properties can the first one own? One or two or even five may be possible, because twenty-five dollars apiece is not a big loss. However, there comes a point when that landlord can no longer continue to lose money. Despite the tax advantages of rental property ownership, you cannot afford a lot of losses, even small ones. How many properties can the landlord who *makes* twenty-five dollars each month on a property own? In theory, as many as he or she wants. You may think you do not want more properties than the one you have, but after implementing some of the money- and time-saving shortcuts in this book, and after putting your rental property on autopilot, you'll see that this job is not so bad after all. You may then want to acquire more properties to further increase your income.

If your rental property loses money, you may think the tax deductions will make up the difference. Although taxes are an important part of a landlord's decision making, you should *never include taxes when determining the real income from a rental property.* After you've computed your taxes, you may have a "profit" for the year, even if you started out with a loss—but because tax laws constantly change, this may *not* be the case next year.

Tax breaks do not make profits.

Consider the following scenario: A landlord makes five hundred dollars a month in rent on a property that costs six hundred dollars a month in expenses. Annualized, that landlord's situation looks like this:

Annual rental income:	$6,000
Annual expenses:	7,200
Annual loss before taxes:	− $1,200

Suppose this landlord's deductible depreciation and mortgage interest add up to more than the loss. At tax time, the landlord finds the following profit picture:

Annual rental income:	$6,000
Annual expenses:	7,200
Annual loss before taxes:	− $1,200
Annual depreciation and interest:	2,000
Annual profit after taxes:	$800

It appears that this landlord is doing fine. All things being equal, he or she can have as many rental properties as desired, since each property makes money at the end of the year even though the properties lose money before all tax deductions are considered.

The only thing you know about the tax laws is that *they will change.* Washington will continue to battle both higher and lower taxes and while it does so, the laws that you begin with this year will not be in effect next year. It would not be prudent for a landlord to base an investment decision on taxes. Always look at your income and expenses *before taxes* when deciding to sell or keep a property. Just because you make a profit this year because of your tax deductions does not mean that you will make a profit next year (after Washington changes the tax laws). The landlord described here is in a fragile situation. If the tax laws change to decrease deductions for depreciation and interest (it happens all the time), this landlord will lose money on the property.

If you are in a similar situation, strongly consider selling the property. When tax laws change against the landlord, as they will at some point (they change back and forth, a juggling act that will never be balanced), fewer people will go into landlording and more landlords will sell their properties. You will be better off selling yours now (if you cannot decrease your expenses or increase your rent), before the tax laws change. Once you get rid of the property, you can search for one that *makes* you money for your hard work.

APPRECIATION IS NICE . . . IF IT OCCURS

Do not justify a losing rental property by thinking that you can sell it for a profit at a later time. As many people found out in the 1980s, there is no rule that guarantees a house will increase in value. Popular thought over the last thirty years was that buying a home was the best investment a person could make. But bank foreclosures and closings proved that a lot of money can be lost from properties that do not appreciate; many owners face properties worth much less today than the day they bought them.

Treat the possibility of appreciation as an added benefit, one that may or may not happen. Do not think that a monthly loss will be made up the day you sell your house.

Nobody knows the future and the future of housing prices is an uncertainty that you cannot risk.

Improving Profits by Lowering Costs

Before selling your home, you can try other alternatives to improving your profit picture. As with a federal deficit, you can either lower spending or raise income to eliminate the loss. Although your renters will not appreciate you raising the rent, you may have to. But before you do, try to lower expenses.

Losing a good tenant is expensive.

Many landlords make raising rents an annual event. This book does not advocate that; its philosophy is *tenant driven*. If your tenants are happy, chances are vastly improved that you will be also. When you practice tenant-driven landlording, you spend time and money up front, by providing a clean, attractive home and getting good tenants. After that, your problems and expenses are minimal. Therefore, if you've taken the time to attract good tenants, the last thing in the world you want is to lose them.

Suppose your tenants pay a monthly rent of $650. If your profit picture shows a loss of $100 a month and you decide to raise the rent to make up for it, you'll find very few tenants willing to accept such an expensive increase, from $650 to $750. If you lose your tenants by raising the rent, it will take over six months to make up the loss of a month's rent (the rent you will lose while finding the next tenant). Avoid this situation. Before tenants move into your rental, make sure that the rent you are asking is reasonable, from your point of view as well as the tenants'. Most people are fair-minded and realistic. Tenants who have rented from you for a long time will understand that you may have to raise rates a little. Costs do increase and they know it. However, do not spring a large increase on your tenants all at once.

Shop around every so often to make sure other homes similar to yours rent for about the same amount. If they rent for more than yours, feel justified in aligning your prices with theirs. If you can beat your competition by renting just below their prices, you will benefit by having lots of happy, paying, long-staying tenants.

REFINANCING

Very few landlords own their rental properties outright. Most have mortgages to pay each month. This is the most expensive cost of owning rental properties. If your mortgage's interest rates are too steep compared to current rates, consider refinancing. When you refinance, you exchange your current high-interest loan for one of lower interest. Sometimes you can lower your monthly mortgage by more than a hundred dollars.

You must fully qualify for a refinanced loan.

Lenders know that you can go elsewhere for a loan, so your current lender will be glad to lower your interest rates. The process is not as easy as it should be, however. Even if your previous payment history at the higher rates is perfect, you must fully qualify for the new loan. Your bank knows that you would have to go through the entire application process if you went elsewhere, so it requires one too, even if you are refinancing an existing loan.

The bank's theory on refinancing is *protection*. They are in a riskier situation than you and they must think about safety. When you obtain a fixed-rate loan, your bank cannot raise your rates. If the loan is at eight percent and interest rates climb to thirty percent, your bank must still accept your payments at the lower rate. However, if rates fall to five percent, you can walk to another bank, get a new loan at the lower rate, and pay off the other one. Therefore, banks take a risk when they give you a fixed-rate loan. They have to do something to make up for this risk every time they loan you money.

When you apply for a new loan with the same lender, it collects a fee for its trouble (processing the application, legal filings, and so forth), and it deserves the fee. The bank also gets a chance to review your current financial situation. Suppose you recently lost your job and no longer qualify for the new loan, even though its payments will be lower than those of your existing one. Your bank will be forewarned.

In most cases, refinancing takes several months. If you've done business with the bank for a long time, it may be able to speed up the process. Do not expect to lower your monthly payments until the final paper is signed on your new loan.

When you apply for refinancing, you will have to pay the application fee *even if you later do not qualify for the loan.* The fee is fair: The mortgage company wants to discourage people from frivolously applying, which simply causes the lender lots of work with no reward. The fee also prevents borrowers from applying at lots of different places at the same time, causing lots of needless work for lenders.

Refinancing makes sense only if you plan to hold the property longer than two years.

By the time your loan is refinanced, you will have spent from $500 to $2,500. Do not let this frighten you;

most lenders roll these fees into the loan itself. Because of the lower interest rate, your monthly payments will be lower than your current payments, even with the added fees. Nevertheless, you do pay the refinancing costs eventually, and they do add to your overall costs. Therefore, a general rule to follow is that refinancing makes sense only if you can get a mortgage that is *two percent lower* than your current one, and only if you plan to keep the property for longer than *two years*. If your mortgage is now twelve percent and you can refinance for eleven percent, the loan costs would make refinancing prohibitive.

But even if you can lower the interest rate by four to five percentage points, refinancing does not make sense unless you will keep the property for more than two years. After two years, the money you save in payments makes up for the refinancing fees.

Consider refinancing the loan for fifteen to twenty years instead of thirty.

When you refinance your mortgage, do not feel that you have to get a thirty-year loan. Because interest rates are the main determinants of monthly payments, you can almost always lower your current payments by refinancing for only fifteen to twenty years. This knocks a few years off the loan, pays off the principal faster (the principal is the amount the house actually costs), and puts more money in your pocket and less in the bank's.

The shorter the loan life (called the "term" of the loan), the more real money you get back when you sell your property. Since you will be paying principal quickly, you own more *equity* (the amount of the home's cost that you have actually paid). More of the selling dollars go back to you when you sell the house.

SHOP AROUND FOR LOANS

Do not feel that you have to use the same bank when you refinance a mortgage you currently hold. As in any other industry, different banks offer different prices on the services they give. Money is a commodity and banks within the same city can offer greatly different interest rates. Most will quote you their current rates over the phone. But banks are not the only institutions that loan money on houses. Look under *mortgage* in the yellow pages for a list of lenders who will be happy to tell you their rates.

A fixed-rate loan is not always the best choice.

The majority of mortgages are fixed-rate loans; that is, their rates cannot rise or fall (except by the refinancing process), no matter what happens to other prevailing rates during the life of the loan. Another popular loan, an *adjustable-rate mortgage* or ARM, offers some advantages over fixed-rate loans.

Adjustable-rate mortgages change over the life of the loan. You could get a mortgage for ten percent, and two years later, you may be paying only eight percent. Of course, the opposite is also true; if rates rise, you could pay as much as the lender feels is competitive with other interest rates at the time. Many view the ARM's changing interest rates as a negative; yet, prices on everything tend to change with time. An adjustable-rate loan is one of the only loans that changes as the economy changes.

Be sure to get an ARM that has a cap on its rate changes. For example, you might find an ARM with a cap of one percent on interest per year and another with a two percent cap. The first one can only increase by a maximum of one percent in any given year; the second can increase as much as two percent. The first loan simplifies budgeting. Some ARMs offer a total rate cap; that is, they have a maximum limit on the interest rate over the life of the loan. For example, a ten percent loan with a twenty percent ceiling will never rise higher than twenty percent no matter what other interest rates do. With a cap, your risk is lower than it would be with no limit.

Rate caps are not the only incentives that banks offer to ARM holders. Generally, ARM rates are one to two percent lower than fixed-rate loans. If your bank currently offers twelve percent mortgages, it probably offers ARMs at ten or eleven percent. More people qualify for ARMs than for fixed-rate loans because the ARM's lower interest rates result in lower monthly payments.

If you still don't know whether to get a fixed-rate or an adjustable-rate loan, you must try to predict what interest rates will do in the future. If you think interest rates will rise (as a result of inflation), then you would prefer a fixed-rate loan, since the interest rate you pay will be locked in for the entire mortgage. If you think rates will drop or stay about the same, you would prefer an adjustable-rate mortgage, since its rate will be lower than that of a fixed-rate loan.

A much larger percentage of home buyers use adjustable-rate mortgages during high-interest times. During the late 1970s and early 1980s, when inflation and interest rates were in the double digits (sometimes mortgage rates went as high as twenty-one percent), people rushed to get adjustable-rate mortgages. During the late 1980s and into the 1990s, fewer people wanted adjustable-rate loans since prevailing interest rates were low compared to the previous decade. No one knows the future, but your expectation of future rates determines which type of mortgage you obtain.

BALLOON MORTGAGES

Some special mortgages have a *balloon payment pro-vision.* These are attractive to borrowers (and refinancers) whose current monthly rental income would not cover a regular loan's payments. Here is the way balloon mortgages work: Suppose you want to borrow or refinance a home worth $150,000. You can get a loan (ten-year or twenty-year; some banks go as high as thirty-year balloon mortgages) for the first $100,000 only. At the end of the loan, you will have a final payment of $50,000 (plus the accrued interest on the $50,000). Balloon loans have many variations, and your banker can help you decide whether one is right for you.

If the final balloon payment frightens you, most lenders let you roll it into an additional loan that you can pay off in time. Even better, if you can afford to pay a higher monthly payment than the actual payment amount, you will pay off the house quicker, and any balloon payment at the end will be much smaller.

Balloon mortgages are useful if you believe your rental income will rise from its current rate. With balloon mortgages, you should do your best to pay any additional money each month on the loan to get the final payment lower. Any time you pay the additional money, be sure the lender credits the extra to *principal* and not to escrow. If the lender puts the extra payment in escrow, the extra money you paid does not go to pay off the loan but is put in a safety fund in case you miss a payment down the road. Although you would eventually get the money back if the bank did not have to use it, you would still have been paying interest on the mortgage amount that the extra money could have been applied to. If you make sure your lender applies the extra money to the principal, you will be paying as little interest as possible throughout the life of the loan.

SHOULD YOU PAY POINTS?

When you obtain or refinance a mortgage, your lender will ask you whether you want to pay *points* on the loan. Points are nothing more than a percentage of your mortgage amount. For example, if you get a mortgage for $175,000, one point would be $1,750 (one percentage point of the full loan).

The idea is this: If you pay one or more points when applying for the loan, you can get a lower interest rate than those who choose not to pay points. For example, here is a typical interest-rate schedule:

Rate	Points
11%	0
10%	1.5
9.5%	3

Given this schedule, if you wanted to borrow $100,000, the interest rate you would pay would automatically be 11 percent. However, if you paid up front a fee of 1.5 percent of the loan ($1,500), you would get the loan for only 10 percent. You could pay three percentage points ($3,000) and get an even lower interest rate (of 9.5 percent). Since the interest rate is such an important determinant of your monthly payment, points can greatly reduce it and thereby increase your monthly cash flow.

Points may be deductible, which further reduces your tax liability.

Although you should check with a competent tax advisor, the points you pay on a mortgage may be deductible as a business expense. It is best if you can deduct them in the first year of the loan, but you may have to amortize them (spread the cost) over the life of the loan. Either way, if points are deductible, it is generally best to pay as many as you can in order to reduce the interest rate you pay over the life of the loan. Some lenders will also let you roll the points into the loan itself, although in this case, you can rarely deduct them in the first year of the loan.

RENTAL OWNERS MAY PAY MORE

Do not be dismayed if the first lender you approach does not want to refinance your loan. Not all lenders offer loans on rental property. Many do; however, they sometimes require a higher interest rate or, more common, require more money down. For instance, one lender may offer a ten percent loan rate with five percent paid down for owner-occupied homes. The same lender may require ten to twenty percent down (money paid in advance) at an eleven percent rate for rental property loans.

Expect this discrimination and be happily surprised if the lender does not charge extra in your case. Actually, lenders have good reason for requiring a little extra from landlords: People buying homes to live in are less likely to default on the loan than people who are buying property to rent. During times of financial duress, landlords are more likely to ignore the mortgage payment on their rental properties than on their own homes. Despite the fact that you are refinancing an existing loan, the lender considers the loan to be brand-new and must protect its own interests.

Tax Advantages for Rental Properties

Although many people dread the thought of rental properties (until they read this book!), almost everybody knows that rental properties offer many tax advantages. The advantages are not as great as they once were, but tax savings play a very important role in your expense and income decisions.

The government wants to encourage the demand for housing. When people buy houses, more money is filtered into the community, builders and suppliers maintain their jobs, and the economy is healthier. To encourage landlords to own properties, the government offers tax incentives that reduce the tax burden on landlords while spurring the rest of the economy. As a rental property owner, tax laws give you more deductions than you get on the home you live in.

DEPRECIATION

Most expenses you incur while owning rental property are deductible business expenses. Even the cost of the home is deductible. However, the Internal Revenue Service does not let you write off the cost of your home in one year (the same holds true for some other items, such as refrigerators). You can only write off a fraction of the house each year, for several years, until you have written it off entirely. This is called "depreciation."

The faster the IRS lets you write off an expenditure, the more money you have in the long run. Since you have to pay fewer up-front taxes because you were able to write things off in the early years, you have more money to invest in other things. A few years ago, the IRS changed the rules so that you now must take longer to write off investment property (twenty-seven-and-a-half years in most cases). The faster depreciation schedules of old (called "accelerated depreciation") are no longer allowed. Therefore, depreciation is not a big advantage for the rental property owner who bought property after 1986.

Depreciation does, however, play an important role when you sell your house. You must *recapture depreciation* when selling the home. Let's say you're losing money on a rental property you bought eight years ago for $100,000, so you sell the house for $100,000. How much profit did you make? You might think you made no profit and therefore owe no taxes; but the IRS knows that you depreciated that property for the eight years you owned it. If you've depreciated $25,000 so far, the IRS thinks that you made a $25,000 profit and wants you to pay taxes on it.

It's to be hoped that the IRS will change the tax laws again to favor faster depreciation. There is talk in Washington that this will happen. Senators and congressmen are finding out that taking tax incentives away from people hampers the economy (a fact that landlords could have told them long ago). Until new rules go into effect, however, depreciation is a nice additional deduction each year, albeit a small one.

EXPENSES AFTER TAX

When you pay for a repair or a light bulb or a utility bill, the price you pay is less than appears at first glance. You should learn to think in terms of *after-tax dollars.* Since each light bulb you purchase is deductible, that light bulb actually costs you less than the price of the bulb.

To find the after-tax cost of any item, you must determine your *marginal tax rate*: the rate (percentage) of taxes you must pay for every dollar you make. Your tax preparer (and as a landlord, you are wise to have one) can tell you your marginal tax rate from last year's tax return.

For example, suppose you are in the twenty-eight percent marginal tax bracket (sometimes just called your "tax bracket"); twenty-eight cents out of every dollar of rent you earn goes to taxes. More important, twenty-eight cents out of every dollar you *spend* is deductible from taxes as well. Therefore, if you know your marginal tax rate, you can compute the true cost of an item with this formula:

after-tax cost = cost × (1.00 − marginal tax rate)

For example, if you are in the twenty-eight percent tax bracket, the $30 sink repair costs you only $21.60 as computed here:

after-tax cost = $30.00 × (1.00 − .28)
giving a result of
after-tax cost = $21.60

The other $8.40 offsets some year-end tax liability. When considering a purchase, learn to think in after-tax dollars to get a true perspective on what the item actually will cost you. (Depending on your withholding, you may not realize the savings until tax time, when you pay fewer taxes; but the tax advantage is really there.)

To compute after-tax income (the amount of income you receive after taxes), you use a similar formula:

$$\text{after-tax income} = \text{income} \times (1.00 - \text{marginal tax rate})$$

Therefore, if a renter pays you $500 in rent, you only realize $360 of it ($500 × .72).

At a glance, it may seem that the after-tax cost and after-tax income cancel each other out. After all, if your true income is actually less than you receive and the money you pay for expenses is less than the money you hand the clerk, is there any reason to ever take after-tax costs into consideration? The answer, as you may have surmised, is yes. Rarely do you have equal income and expenses. You should hope that you have more expenses than income at tax time.

As the beginning of this chapter pointed out, you cannot operate at a loss for very long. However, two tax deductions—interest and depreciation—can easily produce a loss for the year even though your monthly cash flow might still be positive. There is nothing wrong or illegal about these *paper losses*. The IRS gives you the interest and depreciation expenses, even though depreciation is a smaller benefit than it used to be, to encourage you to buy more rental properties.

Until you get close to paying off your mortgage, your interest payments alone will probably offset much of your property's income. When you consider insurance and depreciation as well as the other incidental expenses you incur throughout the year (which are small if you fixed up the home properly), you will almost certainly have a tax loss, even if you made a small "profit" each month when you collected rent. Therefore, you really do pay an after-tax amount for property-related expenses. Your rental income is offset long before you run out of expenses over your many years of property ownership. You pay an after-tax cost on each one of those expenses that exceeds income.

The bigger this paper loss is, the fewer taxes you pay and the more money you have. As long as you are not incorporated, the loss will offset your other income (from your job, interest on savings, or whatever), and you will have much more money to invest elsewhere throughout your landlording career.

Paying the Bills

There are several things a landlord can do to expedite bill paying. One of the newest and easiest is automatic payment of your common monthly bills. For example, your monthly mortgage payment can automatically be deducted from your checking or savings account. Most utility companies now offer this method as well.

Do not fear losing control of these kinds of payments. Several days before the company deducts from your account, you will get a bill that looks just like the bill you always get. Simply write the transaction in your checking account, and on a certain day (always specified on the statement) the company will deduct the amount from your account. If the bill is wrong, you have plenty of time to correct it. If a company deducts more than it said on the statement, they will always correct it (this situation occurs rarely, if ever). Not only do you save the time writing the check, but you save the cost of the check (some carbon-copy checks cost as much as fifteen to twenty cents each) and the stamp. Plus, you know the bill will never be past due and you are free to do something else with your time. Consider automating all your personal bills as well. You can save a few dollars a month in checks and stamps and a lot of time in a year.

You would be surprised at how much a checking account dedicated to your rental business simplifies your tax-time work. Every expense related to the property is recorded, and the checking account ledger makes a good back-up record if you ever get audited. A separate checking account like this keeps you from mixing up business and personal income and expenses. You can still withdraw as much as you want for your own use, since the money is yours (write yourself a check). However, by separating the funds into two accounts you show that you're trying to maintain accurate rental records.

A separate checking account makes tax time much easier.

There is nothing to keep dishonest landlords from mixing money between the two funds. For instance, a dishonest landlord might buy a box of light bulbs for his own home but use a check from the rental property's account. Doing this is highly illegal unless the landlord clearly states on the check register that the funds were for personal use and he does not deduct the light bulbs at tax time. A much better approach is to write a check to yourself, deposit it into your personal account, and write a personal check for the purchase. The IRS knows that separate accounts do not ensure integrity. Nevertheless, maintaining separate checking accounts indicates that you are doing all you can to keep accurate records.

Use the rental property's checking account for all purchases, even cash.

The smart landlords write checks from their property's checking account for *every* transaction they make. Even if you need a single battery for a rental's smoke alarm, write a check for it.

But sometimes you don't want to bother writing a check. Your landlording life would be more difficult if you had to write a check for every small purchase, especially during property renovation. Small cash purchases are known as "petty cash expenses." These purchases are too small to bother with check writing. (You can also pay for large purchases with cash as well, but keep very good records and receipts if you do so, because these cash purchases are more suspect at tax time.) Go ahead and pay cash when necessary and keep all receipts (whether you pay with cash or check). Either keep a log of the cash receipts or keep all the receipts together. Once you have several dollars' worth, do a perfectly legal little trick that accountants have known about for years: Write yourself a check for the amount of the items purchased and put *petty cash* in the memo area. Keep a separate record of the items you bought with cash. Then, deposit the check *back into the property's checking account*. This may seem as though nothing happened; you wrote a check to yourself and deposited it into the same account it was drawn on. However, you now have a checking account record for *every purchase*, even those you paid with cash. This way you can safely find a transaction in the checking account for every single outlay you make on your property.

Be aware that some banks charge extra for a "business" checking account, even though you may write only one or two checks a month on it. Stay away from these added fees. There are many banks who want your business, so find one that offers a no-fee checking account (and preferably one that pays interest on your daily balance as well).

Utilities

LEAVE-ON POLICY

Turning utilities on and off frustrates most landlords. You already know the routine. When your tenant moves out, you must call the utility companies to have the electricity and gas turned on so you can clean and show the home. Not only do you pay for the energy but you pay the connect fee as well. This can be especially frustrating if a tenant leaves in the winter unexpectedly and the pipes freeze because the heat was turned off.

To solve this landlording problem, many utility companies now offer a *leave-on policy*: When a tenant moves out and has the utilities shut off, the utility company automatically transfers the service to your name at a greatly reduced turn-on rate (typically about one-fifth the cost of turning on the utility without the leave-on policy). The utility company then informs you that the utility is in your name. You must register for the policy with the utility company and pay a small one-time fee.

All you have to do when a new tenant moves in is to call the utility company. The company will contact the tenant if the tenant has not yet called, will transfer the billing to the new tenant, and will send you your final bill.

It is nice to know that all future utility turn-ons will be cheaper. It is even nicer to know that your utilities will never actually be turned off again.

ALL-BILLS-PAID POLICY

You may have to decide whether to offer an all-bills-paid policy, especially if your competition does. Generally, you are better off when tenants pay their own utilities. Even the best-intentioned people have a tendency to over-use services they are not paying for, and the costs are extremely unpredictable to you.

A lot of landlords pay water only, leaving the gas and electric to the tenant. This is more common in multi-family dwellings (duplexes, four-plexes, and apartment buildings), because the refuse collection is usually included in the water bill. If a tenant defaults on the water payment, the trash doesn't get picked up for anybody.

Even more likely is that a multifamily dwelling has only one water meter per property instead of per rental unit. If you find yourself in this situation, check with your water company to see how much it costs to put the rental units on separate meters. The cost may be worth the savings in a year or two.

Appliances

Rarely can you rent a property that has no appliances as quickly as one that does. Despite their costs, stoves, ovens, and refrigerators last for many years when purchased new. Also, their after-tax cost is not as great as it would be if you could not deduct the cost from your taxes. (Most appliances require depreciation; you can only deduct part of their cost each year for three to five years.)

Unless your rental is on the expensive side, a stove, oven, and refrigerator are all you need to offer. Tenants seem to clog garbage disposals so often that the repair bills will not justify their benefit in rental appeal. Supplying a washer and dryer is an extremely good rental incentive, but their costs are high and most tenants either buy or rent their own or go to the corner laundry once a week. Install a dishwasher only if competitors do the same. If you want trouble-free landlording, the fewer appliances you have (besides the standard refrigerator, oven, and stove), the fewer trouble calls you will get.

Do not buy extended warranties.

Although each situation is different, most financial experts agree that extended warranties are almost always losing propositions. Your stove may break the day after the original warranty runs out, but the odds are extremely great that it will not. If a stove or range does break, a new heating element usually fixes it right up, and it's inexpensive to replace.

Large appliances are made to last many years with or without extended warranties. If appliances broke a lot, stores could not offer such good-sounding extended warranty deals, so the odds are in your favor if you refuse the extended warranty. Some stores make you initial a legal-looking clause stating that you refused the extended warranty. Don't let this tactic frighten you into purchasing an extended warranty at the last minute.

When buying appliances, buy sizes adequate for the rooms they will occupy. More important, always buy white, no-frills appliances. No matter what color you paint the walls later, the appliances will fit right in.

Look for ads in your local newspaper from discount appliance/stereo dealers offering rock-bottom prices on refrigerators and ranges. (Be sure the refrigerator is frost-free. People sometimes damage freezers by scraping and hammering frost off the freezer walls.) Discount stores generally get people into their stores by advertising the low-priced models, then they attempt to move the customer up to a higher priced model with more features. You want the no-frills, cheap model; other than a few extra dials, these are probably the same on the inside as the more expensive ones. As long as the refrigerator cools and the oven heats, you and your tenants will be happy.

Insurance

Insurance is a very individual thing. Each landlord needs different coverage. There is certainly a plentiful supply of agents around the country who will be very willing to tell you what you need. Consult several before deciding on a policy and choose the one that fits your situation best. The best insurance agents are those who take the time to find out your specific landlording environment and personal needs before telling you which insurance is right for you.

No landlord should be in business who does not have liability insurance, and a million-dollars' worth is okay for a start. In today's litigious society, tenants can sue you for lots of things, many of which may not even seem (and may not be) your fault. Protect your own assets by obtaining liability insurance to cover any negligence or liability suit that you may face.

UMBRELLA POLICIES

Umbrella policies are popular today and offer an inexpensive way to get higher liability coverage. Instead of buying a million-dollar insurance policy, you buy a regular one (it may include property damage, medical coverage, and $100,000 or so of liability) and extend its liability coverage (the *umbrella* that protects you when bad things happen) to a million or more dollars. In most cases, the total you pay will be less than for a full million-dollar policy.

The need for liability coverage cannot be overemphasized. People rarely have enough, so shop around for the best deal and make sure you are amply covered. The loss of a life is difficult to put a price on (but whatever it is, you can bet it will be huge), and your peaceful rest at night is worth the price of liability protection.

If you own bare land on which you may someday build rental property, buy liability insurance for it as well. Children playing on your land can hurt themselves. Even if they should not have been on the property in the first place, you can still be charged with negligence.

Periodically review insurance policies, agents, and companies.

You might have the best insurance agent in the world, but you should still shop around every year or so to see whether another company offers better values. Don't spend a lot of time looking (you don't have to call every company in the phone book), but call four or five to see what is out there. Insurance policies are just contracts, and most of them are very similar. Remember that your agent is completely out of the picture if you ever have a claim (an adjuster steps in to handle the proceedings), so don't base a company solely on a nice agent.

HOW MUCH PROPERTY INSURANCE?

Once you have enough liability to cover disastrous situations, you must decide how much property coverage you need. That is, if your home burned down, how much would you need to replace it?

There is no easy answer to this question, but your insurance agent should be able to help. However, make sure you get *full replacement coverage*. Without it, you will only get the depreciated value of your losses. In other words, the insurance will pay only a few dollars for the five-hundred-dollar refrigerator you bought five years ago, if you lost it in a fire. But if you have full replacement, the insurance will cover the full cost of a new, comparable model at today's prices.

Generally, you save much more money if you maintain high deductibles.

Ask your insurance agent for the cost of insurance at each deductible level. A policy with $250 deductible is typically much more expensive than one with $1,000 deductible. As a review, suppose a small fire ruined $3,000 worth of your home. If you had a $250 deductible, your insurance company would pay you $2,750, since the first $250 is on you. If you had a $1,000 deductible, insurance would only pay you $2,000.

Obviously, the smaller deductible means you get more if you have a claim. However, in most cases the price of lower deductibles is relatively high. Your insurance company does not want to bother with small claims, so a higher deductible means you will not be going to them for petty damages, since you will have to foot so much of the first few dollars (the deductible). Don't sweat the small losses. The money you save in premiums is almost always worth large deductibles. Besides, the more small losses you claim, the higher the company will raise your rates; the small losses are simply not worth the expenditure.

One person's small loss or large deductible is different from another's. Ask your agent to show you the price of your property coverage at each deductible level and then decide whether the marginal differences are worth the added costs. Since your losses are tax deductible, large deductibles make even more sense; you can subtract the amount of the deductible from your taxable income.

You may need less property coverage than you think.

Feel free to second-guess your agent when buying property coverage. You will probably need less than the agent first prescribes, if he or she suggests that you insure the property for its current selling price; the cost of replacing damaged or even "totaled" property is never as high as the selling price of the property. If your home is brick, or partially brick, remember that bricks don't burn, and they will not need replacing after a fire. You also cannot lose the land the home sits on (the land is part of the cost of the home).

If you have done your job—installed smoke alarms and a fire extinguisher—chances are much improved that a small fire stays small. There is nothing you can do to avoid every catastrophe, but if you objectively look at the odds against a total loss, you will see that you need less coverage than first appears.

Some landlords have *no* property coverage. Rental property coverage is generally higher than that on owner-occupied homes. Some landlords feel that a complete loss is rare and not even worth the premium for property coverage. You have to do your own math and take your own chances in this situation. Consider how many years of premiums it takes to buy a replacement home (or fix yours if completely damaged) and then decide. Whatever you do, have adequate liability protection. Also, make sure to recommend, in writing if possible, that your tenants get renter's insurance. Tenants should understand that your insurance does not cover their possessions in the event of a loss. Renter's insurance is cheap, but most renters fail to buy it even when advised to do so.

PAYING THE PREMIUMS

A surprising number of landlords get year-long insurance policies and pay for them in monthly installments. They use part of their monthly rent to pay for that month's premium. Although this seems easiest at first (and the insurance companies prefer this), there is almost always a small service charge added to each payment. If you pay the full annual premium at once, you do not get the service charges. If you add up how much you pay in service charges over the year, you will find that it's a large percentage of the annual premium.

If you have a difficult time paying your full year's premium in advance, get a small loan from your bank. Generally, the interest rate on a small short-term loan will be less than the service charge on your monthly premium. During the year, put a portion of your rent in a savings account so that the next year you can pay the policy in full and have some money left over.

Summary

No landlord can stay in business if he or she is losing money on the property. Rental properties make money if owned and managed the right way. This chapter showed you how to maximize the profits and minimize the losses. With very few exceptions, a losing property should make money or should be sold. There are too many good rental houses waiting for a caring landlord such as yourself to waste time and money on a losing house.

CHAPTER NINE

Thinking About Landlording?

THE POSITIVE SIDE of landlording shines through-out this book, as you learn how to streamline your efforts. You've read how to save time and money as well as how to attract and keep good tenants. Most of you are landlords already. But several of you, although interested in rental properties, have not yet taken the plunge because you have doubts or fears.

This chapter attempts to answer the questions of would-be landlords. Even though most of your questions have probably been addressed in earlier chapters, there are many other things you should know before leaping into the landlording business. This chapter gives you an over-view of some of the things you can expect.

The Problems

If you own rental property long enough, you are bound to encounter problems: You will get tenants who do some (or maybe a lot) of damage to your home. You will get tenants who move out in the middle of the night, leaving you nothing but a bad check. At times, you will curse your landlording responsibilities and want to bail out.

People have many reasons for not becoming landlords. The difficulties described above are only two of the reasons. But remember: If you have heard of someone's landlording nightmares, chances are excellent that the landlord did not take the time to prepare the home right and to attract good tenants. Also remember that bad news travels much faster than good. The horror stories you hear about rarely happen. Bad tenants will come and go, but you will have more good than bad. Although you cannot guarantee this, you can stack the odds in your favor (as you've already seen). Nevertheless, even the best landlords sometimes experience rental property grief.

It takes landlording savvy to minimize problems. If it didn't, the competition would be fierce and rents would be much lower.

So if you are doomed from the start to have problems, *why* bother to become a landlord? If caring landlords were to list the benefits they derive from their properties, in most cases the advantages would outweigh the drawbacks. Of course, if landlording were easy and trouble-free, everybody would do it. The simple truth is that landlording really is easier than most people think, which is why you should consider it. Your tenants will not view you as the big bad landlord if you treat them with respect. Many tenants and landlords become very good friends.

If you prepare the home well and find good tenants, you'll rarely even see your rental house. The rent comes promptly in the mail each month and most of the tenants' calls are easy to handle. But suppose trouble does break out, say a heater fails in the middle of winter. Which tenant is going to be the most patient and appreciative of a landlord's promptness and which is going to threaten to move out: the tenant living in a run-down home who never got a good look at the landlord, or the tenant who knows that the landlord cares about the tenant and the tenant's family? The answer is obvious.

Do not sweat the problems. Learn to stack the odds in your favor. Go into your landlording career with a positive attitude. And be determined that you'll let the home sit empty for three months before you'll rent to someone with an inadequate income or a poor rental history. Landlords with this attitude often have lots of qualified people wanting the home; their biggest "problem" is having to choose among the many hopefuls.

You cannot predict every problem, but you certainly can learn from each one.

You are going to face situations that you never would have imagined before becoming a landlord. Tenants will try to use the furnace in the sweltering heat of summer (after you turned off the pilot light in the spring). They will remove dirty air conditioner filters without replacing them with clean ones. They will miss appointments with you or send you an extra five dollars in the rent check for no apparent reason (tell them about their mistake). Tenants will lock themselves out, lose their key, move their relatives in, and mow only half the yard.

Your problems will not only come from tenants. Seeing your success, your friends or cousins might want to go into the rental property business. They will want all your advice free of charge. They'll also want you to "show" them how to fix up their house (you do the work, all the while adding to the competition).

Since you cannot predict every disaster, annoyance, or happy event, do not try to. When something goes wrong, analyze the situation during and after it passes. Decide the best way to keep that problem from recurring.

Landlording does not have to take much of your time. Expect to invest the most time and money at the beginning of your landlording career, when you spruce up the property and get good tenants. You can usually find tenants you want in only a few hours, at the open house (remember to beat your competitor's price and would-be tenants will come in droves). The new tenant interview takes another hour.

Be realistic. There is no way you can be an absentee landlord and still expect your home to remain standing. Day-to-day landlording does take some time—but much of it is on the phone with tenants rather than visiting them personally. You'll spend the rest of your time on routine tasks such as utility turn-on calls, depositing rent checks, and the like. Expect landlording to be a part-time job, because that is what it is. You can streamline the job, however, to be the most rewarding and the most "part-time" job of your life.

The Money

Rental properties can make you a lot of money. As discussed in the last chapter, you can improve your profit picture greatly by following a few simple procedures and by regularly checking out the competition. Most landlords rarely do the latter, but they should. *Know thine competing landlords and you will trump their every move.*

Most new landlords are thrown into landlording without wanting it. They inherit a home or get stuck with an extra house that will not sell (this is especially true in depressed housing markets, when homes may sit for months without being sold). Some of these reluctant landlords learn to cope with their newfound investment properties. And once they see the positive side of landlording, they start searching for more houses to buy.

Many good landlords buy additional properties the longer they are in the business.

The amount of money you can make obviously varies from situation to situation. Returns of thirty percent and higher are very reasonable, and unlike many fixed-rate investments, your profits should increase over time. When that fateful day arrives—when you pay off the mortgage and have the rental income *all* to yourself—you will wonder why everybody is not a landlord.

BUYING THE RIGHT PROPERTY

The primary determinant of your rental profit is the amount of the mortgage payment. The best way to lower monthly payments is to buy the home at a good price. Once you do, find the best interest rate available and then refinance (described in the last chapter) whenever rates fall by two percent or more. Lowering the payment always increases your profit picture. (Those of you who inherit a mortgage-free house are way ahead in the income game!)

Do not go overboard in the purchase. Too many hopeful landlords make the following dramatic mistake: They buy a nice home in a nice area for a good price. There doesn't seem to be anything wrong with that so far. A nice home needs very little fixing up or money and should rent quickly. But the problem is that the owner made the mistake of getting a "good buy" as if he or she were going to live in the house instead of buying it to rent out. Read on to find out why this is a mistake.

Search for a structurally sound house that is in good physical shape outside but looks terrible inside and out and is located in a clean, safe, owner-occupied neighborhood. Buy the worst-looking house on the block and turn it into the best-looking one. (Chapter 10 gives you more insight on buying rental properties and Chapter 11 explains some ways to fix them up inexpensively.)

Bad-looking houses in good neighborhoods sell *far below* their actual value, in most cases. For some strange reason, owners and landlords alike rarely want to consider buying such a house. But smart landlords know that a bad-looking house can be made to look good and that as long as the structure is sound, the cosmetics are easy to fix. If you are wondering how to find these kinds of properties, select the five lowest priced houses in your newspaper's "For Sale" section, find the one with the best location, and you've probably found an ideal rental property.

Four $30,000 houses are much better than one $120,000 house.

Keep in mind that it's always better to own four inexpensive properties than one expensive one. Suppose you live in a part of the country where $120,000 buys a nice two- or three-bedroom house. That house will bring in around $850 a month in rent. (Adjust these numbers upwards or downwards to fit your area.) But if you buy four houses for $30,000 (you would buy them one at a time, of course) and fix them up, you could expect about $450 a month from each of them. That comes to $1,800 in rent. Compare that with the $850 for the one house and you'll see that you've more than *doubled* your rental income. By buying cheap houses and fixing them up you can make considerably more money than if you take the easy route, buying one "nice" house that can demand a higher purchase price.

In theory (and one of the rules of thumb in real estate), a rental house should rent for one percent to two percent of its total purchase price. Therefore, if you buy a house for $50,000, it should rent for $500 to $1,000; quite a wide range, but the location determines which extreme is closest. The problem with this theory is that the more expensive a rental house is, the less rent it generates *in proportion* to its price.

It is very difficult to convince people that cheaper rentals are the way to make a lot of money. They don't see that the time they spend fixing up a run-down house pays for itself over and over. Even if they hired out all the renovation work, in the vast majority of cases they would still come out ahead. Please remember this important fact:

> No matter how nice a home is, there comes a point when you cannot ask for more rent. Those who can afford the higher rent would much rather buy their own home.

The more you ask in rent, the fewer renters you will have. The reverse is also true: Cheaper rent broadens your rental base and provides lots more qualified renters. In addition, the math is on your side. A cheaper home generates *much* more rent in proportion to its purchase price than an expensive home. That is why four $30,000 houses generate tremendously more rental income than one $120,000 home. Seldom can a $120,000 house generate $1,200 a month in rent (one percent of its purchase price). If your local housing and rental prices are higher or lower, adjust the numbers and you will reach the same conclusion.

Vacancies hurt much less when you own inexpensive houses.

During the months a property is vacant, you can much more easily afford the mortgage payment on a $30,000 house than on a $120,000 house. Landlords should estimate that their properties will be occupied eleven months out of the year. (Generally, for caring landlords, this is too conservative because their tenants tend to stay longer.) During the vacant months, you will have to pay the mortgage as always, tenant or no tenant, and you will wish you owned a cheaper home when that payment comes out of your own pocket. Also, when you own four $30,000 houses, the income from the other three makes up for the loss of rent on one.

This scenario illustrates the point that cheaper houses bring in a much greater percentage of rent than more expensive ones. Do not even think about starting off with four houses at once, but do consider the advantages of cheaper homes and look for them when you search for properties; you can turn a diamond in the rough into a desirable and profitable rental.

FINANCING

Most of the information in the last chapter about refinancing applies to funding new loans as well. Search around for the best rate because different institutions offer vastly different interest rates.

Be wary of financing schemes that use mirrors (and fine print) to hide their subtleties.

Although there are times when a standard mortgage is not the best way to go, in most cases it usually is (unless you can pay cash). The midnight cable television channels are filled with real estate get-rich-quick schemes and fancy financing tricks that require you to buy their notebooks and videos before you can share in the wealth. Most of these schemes work in theory but are very difficult to execute in practice. They require equity sharing (making the tenant a part-owner) or heavy, multilayered debt, which you do not need.

Not all of these purchase schemes are bad, but remember that there is no free lunch in this world. By far the best "scheme" to becoming a successful landlord is to do as this book suggests: Buy a house cheaply, fix it up well, and rent it for a healthy return.

That said, there *is* one financing trick that can work. It not only pays for the house and its renovation but also puts money in the landlord's pocket. (Before putting this plan in action, talk with a tax advisor and banker; in most cases, they will see nothing wrong with the idea.) Assuming you find a great buy on a house (you should not buy otherwise), take out a nonmortgage loan, at a higher interest rate if necessary, for the rental house's purchase price and fix-up costs. You can sometimes get a home equity loan on the house you live in to cover the rental's purchase and renovation.

For example, suppose you find an incredible deal: a house that nobody wants (except you) for $25,000. The house paint is peeling, the trash in the yard needs shoveling, the weeds reach the roof's loose shingles, and the inside walls and floors haven't seen paint and carpet for three generations. Because they take pride in their neighborhood, the neighbors have begun condemnation proceedings. Your knowledgeable eye looks past the peeling paint to see that the floors are solid and the structure sound. You know that in about two months you will be those neighbors' best friend and hero.

If you can, find a way other than a mortgage to get the $25,000 purchase price and an additional $2,000 to $4,000 for fixing up the house. It really does not matter how you borrow the funds as long as you do not get a mortgage. Mortgages take several months to get and require a lot of fees up front. You can better use that time and money to fix up the house. To get such a loan, you may have to pay a higher interest rate. Do not worry about the rate you pay — you will pay off this loan in two or three months and the interest for such a short time is negligible.

Some people get a *single-pay note* for three months. This is a short-term loan whose interest and full principal are due at the end of the three months (or whatever the term of the loan happens to be). If you have to use credit card money, do so. The price of the house should be small enough so that you can get the funds.

Once you buy the house, spend the next two months renovating it. Improving the cosmetics improves the value of a home tremendously. Installing shutters, new shingles, new electrical outlets and circuits if needed, refurbishing the plumbing if needed, painting, carpeting, and mini-blinds can easily turn a $25,000 house into one worth $60,000 to $75,000.

Once you finish the renovation, get a mortgage on the property. This mortgage does two things: It lowers the interest rate you pay (crucial to getting the rental income to exceed your loan payment) and it gets rid of that short-term loan.

The key to this financing method is determining how much the mortgage amount should be. You might think that the mortgage should equal the balance of the short-term loan, but you can get much more than that now. Remember that over the previous two to three months you created lots of equity by renovating the home. Most lenders will mortgage as much as sixty percent to eighty percent of a home's *market value*. If your rental house is now worth $65,000 after renovation, you can get a mortgage for $39,000 to $52,000. When you pay off the $30,000 or so of the short-term loan plus interest, you are left with $9,000 to $24,000 in your pocket!

This financing method may appear to be just another of those fancy schemes paraded on television and at real estate investment seminars. But the only "catch" is that you somehow have to get that first short-term loan. This is made easier because you do not care how much the interest rate for that loan will be. The higher the rate you are willing to pay, the more lenders are willing to loan you the money. Also, you can use your own cars and current home as collateral for the short-term loan if you have faith in your abilities to be a caring landlord. You will be successful at landlording if you want to be; and even if you hire professionals to help you with the renovation of your first rental home, you will soon have the rent rolling in, making those payments for you, in less than five months from the first day you began.

The money you put in your pocket from the mortgage makes the monthly mortgage payment higher than if you'd gotten a lesser amount. The rent money should cover, or almost cover, the mortgage each month. If you need to use some of the extra money to make a few mortgage payments, do so. After several months, you can decide whether you want to roll the money into another rental or apply it to the loan to pay it off faster. Either way gives you the capital to invest in a second home even though you only have one mortgage. If you decide to buy a second home, you can pay for most of it with the extra money from the first home's loan. The two houses' incomes will let you pay off the mortgage very quickly.

Tax Benefits

The tax benefits of landlording are very good, even though they are not as good as they once were. Landlords who actively manage their own homes (as opposed to passive real-estate trust investors who never see the homes they invest in) enjoy tax deductions that offset their income from other sources.

You can enjoy tax benefits the first month you buy the rental.

You do not have to wait until tax time to enjoy rental tax savings. Once you buy rental property, go to a trustworthy tax advisor to find out how to maximize your income by minimizing your taxes. If you are employed, the tax advisor can perform a quick analysis of your records to see how many exemptions you can now claim on your job. By raising the number of exemptions (you must fill out a W-4 form; the tax advisor will tell you exactly what to do), you can increase your take-home pay each paycheck instead of having to wait until year-end to enjoy the tax advantages.

Kinds of Ownership

When going into any business, you have the right to form one of three kinds of ownerships: a *single proprietorship*, a *partnership*, or a *corporation*. (There are a few other legal entities possible, but these three are the most common.) Their differences lie primarily in their tax advantages and also in the way expenses and income are divided between the investors.

The single proprietorship is the most common method small landlords use to buy rental property. You are a single proprietor if you buy your own rental house, fix it up yourself (and hire help if needed, of course), and receive the income from the house. The house will be taxed at your personal tax rate. Although you must fill out an extra page or two on your tax form each year (Schedule C), the IRS treats rental income as ordinary income. The disadvantage to the sole proprietorship is its liability: You are fully responsible and liable for any and all decisions made regarding the property. If you are sued for negligence, your personal assets are at risk.

Partnerships are simply proprietorships between two or more people. No special tax consideration is given (although a lot more tax work is necessary, as described in the next section). The biggest advantage to partnerships over sole proprietorships is that your liability is limited to half that of sole proprietorships. If you are sued, you are responsible for half the damages.

Corporations receive special tax treatment and liability protection. The corporate owners of a property are not personally responsible for damages. In most cases, only the corporation is responsible for damages. Therefore, in the case of a large lawsuit, the assets of the corporation may be lost (the house and any funds the corporation owns), but the owner's personal assets remain untouched. Here is a summary of the three types of business ownership:

Type of Ownership	Liability
Sole proprietorship	Owner is fully responsible.
Partnership	Owners are partially responsible.
Corporation	Liability is limited to the corporation's assets only.

Do not let this discussion of lawsuits frighten you. If you are a caring landlord who follows the landlording laws of your state, you will probably never face a lawsuit. The types of ownership, however, warrant discussion, since something other than a sole proprietorship may be best for your specific situation.

PARTNERSHIPS

Many landlords, especially first-time ones, fear going it alone. They prefer to have a partner. There is nothing inherently wrong with getting a partner. The two of you can share the expenses, get loans more easily, and work only half as hard. Despite the benefits, consider the disadvantages of a partnership before jumping into one.

To keep things legal and clean, the first step partners must take is recording their partnership at the county clerk's office. The partnership is then considered by the state to be a legal entity, entitled to own property and to receive income. You should then consult an attorney to write a *partnership agreement*. This explains how the two of you will share in the investment (typically half-and-half, although the division can be whatever the two of you agree to); it also dictates the divisions of labor and contains clauses that specify how you will divide the assets if one or both of you ever want out of the partnership.

Tax time is much more difficult for partnerships than for sole proprietorships. In addition to your regular personal tax forms, the partnership itself must file tax forms, including a balance sheet and an income statement. Your tax preparer can do the extra paperwork, but you are out money for the preparer's time.

A good deal for two is usually a better deal for one. Rarely does a good rental property require a partnership.

Not only do you divide the expenses between you and a partner but you divide your income and tax benefits as well. Depreciation, deductions, and rent have to be shared according to the terms of the partners' original agreement. As you have seen throughout this book, rental property can be easy to manage. There is simply no reason to get a partner for one rental house. If you owned fifty houses, a partnership might make more sense (although incorporation would probably produce more advantages, as explained below). But even then, a good deal for a partnership is an even better deal for a single person since that person keeps all the benefits.

As many partners have found out, owning the property yourself is actually *easier* at times than owning with a partner. Invariably, one partner's heart is not into the job as much as the other's. Instead of risking hard feelings between friends, it makes much more sense to venture out on your own, keeping your properties separate and your friendships intact.

INCORPORATION

A corporation is simply a legal entity that can own income-producing businesses. To create this legal entity, you must file corporation papers with your state. Because of some legal advantages, many people prefer to file in the state of Delaware. You can do this by mail. An attorney can help you incorporate your rental property. Because there are several ways to incorporate, you might want to check the methods available so you can decide which is right for your specific situation and for the state in which you want to incorporate.

Although not necessarily a substitute for up-to-the-minute legal advice, your local library has books that describe how anyone can incorporate. Incorporation requires nothing more than filing some forms and paying a fee. If you are a do-it-yourselfer, you can save a lot of attorney fees by incorporating yourself.

Although people tend to link the term *corporation* with large businesses, anybody can incorporate any business. A corporation may consist of only a single owner, a group of two or three people, or more. The corporation simply acts as a legal protective blanket, so that your liability is limited only to your assets *inside* the corporation. In most cases, if a problem arises from the business, your personal assets cannot be touched.

Although the tax laws are not as generous to corporations as they once were (thus slowing down the economy and the housing market as well), corporations still enjoy some tax benefits over the other forms of ownership. As an officer of the corporation, however, you are actually taxed twice. Not only does the corporation pay taxes on its income, but you must pay additional taxes on any money you receive from the corporation (called "dividends"). This drawback limits some of the tax advantages you receive as a single owner in a corporation.

The other drawback to incorporation is its paperwork. At tax time you must file many papers; additionally, you may need to file other papers throughout the year. Again, a tax preparer can help you with all this, but you are out the cost for the preparer's time. Limiting your liability by incorporating has the cost of less income, fewer tax deductions, and more paperwork.

Despite its drawbacks, incorporation makes a lot of sense. One lawsuit can devastate you in this litigious society. Incorporation greatly limits your risk. Because of the limited risk, you may be able to get by with less liability insurance than you would otherwise. If this makes you uncomfortable, talk with an attorney before changing your insurance policy after incorporating.

Kinds of Rental Properties

Single-family houses make attractive rental units for a lot of landlording investors. The tenants take care of the yard in most cases, and you can be proud of renovating a run-down home. Single-family homes offer renter advantages as well. The tenants can have pets (depending on your regulations and the size of your yard), a garage, and privacy, three things not always available in multitenant housing (like apartments).

If you buy the right properties—that is, if you buy *cheap* properties in good areas—the rent you charge for your house can be competitive with apartments in the area (another reason not to buy an expensive home that is already fixed up). With competitive rent and the other physical advantages to single-family housing, you should never worry about a shortage of tenants.

Never rule out a chance to buy an inexpensive duplex, four-plex, or small apartment building. The advantages of rental properties increase the more units there are on the property. Leave the large apartment complexes to the big shots, because these kinds of properties pose problems beyond the scope of most beginning investors. They require on-site maintenance and management; and in certain areas of the country, rent control is more likely.

*Multifamily housing is generally easier to manage
and produces higher returns than several single-
family houses. That is why you see so many apartment
buildings.*

Tenants do not always want to care for a lawn. Typically, you the landlord are responsible for a lawn when
you own a duplex or any multifamily housing (although
you may be able to require tenants to take care of their part
of the lawn). Find a trusty neighborhood kid to mow the
lawn weekly if you do not want to do it. Although single-
family housing offers a lot of tenant advantages, demand
for multifamily units still remains high, so the advantages
to you are tremendous.

Suppose you own a little building consisting of four
rental units. One trip takes care of four houses! When
renovating the place, it is much easier and cheaper to
renovate the one property than four separate houses. The
building only has one roof. The outside walls need less
paint than the walls of four separate houses. Insurance is
less. The heating and air conditioning units are the same
and take the same size filters. The shutters, miniblinds,
and so forth are the same size for each unit. Any type of
repair or replacement is automatically easier because the
units are identical.

The biggest advantage to multifamily housing is its
cost. A duplex *rarely* costs twice as much as two houses of
the same size as one unit of the duplex. In most instances,
a duplex is only slightly more expensive than *one* house.
You can buy a duplex, renovate one of its units, get a rent-
paying tenant in, and take your time (and the tenant's
money) to fix up the other unit. The more units per building (from duplex, to three-plex, to four-plex, and so on), the
lower the individual cost of each unit.

In some areas of the country, mobile homes make
attractive rental units as well. They are generally *much
less expensive* than houses, especially used mobile homes

(the best kind), and their renovation generally costs much less. The best thing about them is that they demand almost as much rent as a comparable apartment. In other words, a two-bedroom mobile home should bring you almost as much rent as a two-bedroom apartment.

Landlords lucky enough to have made the mobile home plunge have been rewarded with higher returns than they otherwise would have. There are drawbacks, however. Mobile homes do not appreciate as much as regular homes. When you buy one and renovate it, the renovation is worth less than it would have been had you fixed up a run-down house. Banks are not as apt to loan money on mobile homes and insurance is generally higher for them.

Not only do financing and insurance cost more, a mobile home does not last as long as a house, and you must find a space, with utility hookups, for the mobile home to stay. Generally, you must rent a mobile home pad in a mobile home park. However, if you have a vacant lot that is zoned for mobile homes, you can often get utility attachments installed on the property.

Organization Is the Key

Once you become a landlord, you must keep accurate records of all your expenses and all your income. Keep all receipts as a back-up and be able to justify any expense you make. Landlords are no more suspect for audit than anyone else, but there is always a chance the IRS will want to review your records.

If you are the kind of person who dislikes detailed record keeping, get organized quickly. Actually, record keeping is relatively easy. Keep a journal in your car; every time you make a purchase, enter it in the journal. Remember also that you can deduct mileage that is directly related to all rental property activities, so write the beginning and ending mileage for each trip as well.

Chapter 12 describes such record keeping in more detail. You don't need a computer for your first time as a landlord; all you really have to do is keep an up-to-date journal of your expenses.

Summary

Many first-time landlords go through the following stages: fear during the purchase, regret in the middle of renovation, pride at the end of renovation, and joy when depositing their first rent check. After that, they wonder why they did not buy a rental property earlier (well, the caring ones do). It is a nice feeling to know that someone else (your tenant) is buying a house for you.

You can get rich in landlording, but it happens at a slow and steady rate rather than overnight.

Return on a smart landlord's investment usually outpaces that of other investments by a large margin. The tax advantages are great as well. Owning rental property will not make you an instant millionaire, but it will offer you a steady income and will outpace inflation by a large margin, in most cases.

If you are considering landlording, make sure you buy the right properties. Keep your sights *low*; as this chapter pointed out, buying several cheaper properties makes you a lot more money than one expensive one (and they are easier to keep rented as well). Cosmetically bad but structurally sound houses in good neighborhoods are gold to the smart investor. The buy-low/high-return rule multiplies if you consider multiunit housing such as duplexes and four-plexes.

The kind of house you buy and the type of business entity you become are important decisions you must make, but not the most important for success. The most important part of landlording is emphasized throughout this book: Be courteous to your tenants, treat them like good customers as long as they fulfill their part of the agreement, offer them a clean, attractive home in a safe neighborhood, and you will be more successful than you ever thought you could be in this business.

CHAPTER TEN

Finding and Buying More Properties

ONCE YOU BECOME a successful landlord, you should duplicate that success. After putting one property with good tenants on autopilot, start looking for another to increase your return even more. Finding new properties to buy is fairly easy, but you must maintain control. The price you pay has got to be as low as possible in order to offer fair and competitive rent and still reap a large return on your investment.

This chapter explores ways to find and buy rental properties. There are always good deals out there but you have to look for them. This chapter deviates slightly from the advice in the previous ones. Instead of offering immediate hands-on advice, it attempts to teach you how to approach the business of home buying from an investor's point of view. In different parts of the country, buying a house, even an investment house, requires different strategies; this chapter does not attempt to cover them all. But by the time you finish this chapter, you will feel more confident in your buying approach and you will be able to strike a better bargain than may have otherwise been possible.

Buying rental properties means finding more than *good* deals, it means finding *great* deals. Set your buying sights *lower* and do not be afraid to walk away from a deal you wanted. There is always another one right around the corner.

Filter Through the Hype

Rarely should you look for an investment property in your Sunday newspaper's "Homes on Parade" color supplement. The more money spent on advertising a house, the more money it must bring to pay for that advertising. Investors find good rental properties by reading the small hidden ads, the ads that read like the one displayed in this section.

**For sale: 3-bedroom, 1 bath, garage. 12 West Pine Road.
$40,000 or best offer. Call Bill at 555-9382.**

A home such as this probably looks terrible. It almost certainly needs painting and renovating. The price is low (and Bill obviously couldn't spend much money for the ad). Investors like the fact that Bill announces he is taking offers. Although you should negotiate every home you buy, Bill is telling everyone that he needs to sell quickly and would consider taking much less than the asking price.

This type of ad does not guarantee anything. Bill may be a slick real estate agent who does not even have a $40,000 house; he just wants to gather as many names of buyers as possible so he can "move them up" to higher priced homes. Most real estate agents would never be this devious, but you should approach all real estate transactions with caution and with one goal in mind: buying the cheapest house you can, in a good neighborhood, that will be attractive to renters.

Look for your price first, then the address, then the home.

When first looking through newspaper ads for a house, ignore everything but the price. Set a maximum amount that you will pay. There is no one right price for the entire country. For instance, in parts of Oklahoma and elsewhere in the Midwest, at present you can buy a two- or three-bedroom house for as little as $15,000. In Hawaii, the same "great deal" would be around $50,000. Whatever the rock-bottom prices are for your area, stick with the bare minimum that *fixer-up* houses sell for.

A good strategy (mentioned in the previous chapter) is to choose the five lowest priced houses in the newspaper. If you have no idea how low the prices can go, choosing the lowest five will teach you a lot. Do this for several weeks and you will become an expert at low-priced housing in your area.

Only after finding the cheapest houses, then and *only* then look at the addresses. Since you narrowed the search to the most important buying consideration, price, you can now look for the second most important attribute: location. Attempt to find houses that are located in good neighborhoods. If you see a house in an unsafe neighborhood, cross it off the list. If you see a house in a neighborhood that floods every other week, cross it off the list.

Only after finding cheap houses in good neighborhoods should you consider looking any further. Relax and enjoy the search. Treat it as a hobby. You may not find a good investment deal the first week you start looking. You may not find one for many months. You will, however, run across a good deal eventually, and you will be surprised at how inexpensively you can purchase such a home.

The houses you are interested in are not the ones realtors push with pictures and fancy descriptions. The houses you are interested in do not make high commissions for realtors, which is why realtors do not take the time with them that they do with much more expensive houses.

Investors' Secrets

Rental property investors obey a few rules. Over the years, you will pick up some of your own. Rather than attempt to give you an exhaustive list of "house-buying tips," this section will present some of the more common philosophies that underlie the buying of property. Buying a rental house for investment reasons is very different from buying a house for your family to live in forever and ever. The goal of the investor is always to maximize his or her return. But to be a hands-off landlord, not only price but the location of the property and the home's fix-up potential are almost equally important—because you want to provide a home that both you and your tenants will be proud of.

GET THE PRICE LOWER

Everybody who offers a house for sale, no matter how much or little the asking price, expects to bargain. If a house sells for $500,000, the owner knows that he or she will get less before the final deal is made. The same holds for a house selling for $15,000. The asking price actually means very little except to put a cap on the highest price you would pay for this house.

Do not even think about making an offer on a house until you have seen it. Even then, it is best to first walk away, leaving the seller wondering if you ever will make an offer. Never mention anything about price the first time you look at the house.

Offend the seller with your first offer.

You are being a wise investor when you attempt to get the asking price much lower. Do not fear offending the seller. As a matter of fact, your goal *should be* to offend the seller with your offer. You need to see just how far this seller is willing to go before he or she will part with the house. You are not out to win a personality contest, and if you go too low, the seller will simply tell you that the price is unreasonable and either make a counteroffer or tell you to find a house that is more in your price range. Many investors have been turned down on a low offer, only to be called a few days later with an acceptance. Of course, you then would be less interested and should make an even lower offer to see what happens. You can always move back up if your first offer was reasonable.

Remember that verbal real estate contracts are not binding. (Verbal contracts other than real estate contracts are binding.) To be a valid offer, you must submit it in writing. If you work with the seller directly, you can mention your verbal offer to see how he or she responds, but most sellers rightly expect all offers in writing. A real estate contract for purchase is available at any local office supply store and is relatively easy to fill out. Buy several of them. You might make ten offers on ten properties before getting one accepted. If you have a friend in real estate (everyone knows *somebody* in real estate), your friend can help you fill out your first real estate offer-to-buy contract.

To effectively buy investment properties, you need to be able to bargain. This means you must be able to look at a house with as much disdain as possible, no matter how great a deal it seems. When walking through the house, say absolutely nothing positive about it. Point out every negative flaw you can find. Do not commit yourself in any way to the possibility of offering something the seller might consider reasonable.

You are doing this as much for yourself as for the seller. It is too easy to get wrapped up in one house, deciding that it is *the* house you want to buy, before you get the price nailed down. Being disdainful is not being cruel, although at first this approach may not come easily to you. If you walk away from this house without buying it, there will be another one, even better, that you will find later. When buying property, especially low-priced property that nobody seems to want, you hold all the cards.

LOCATE THE PREVIOUS SELLING PRICE

Land records are public information. The most important tool you can have in your investor's utility belt is an understanding of the land records at your county courthouse. Given the address of any house in your county, you can go to the courthouse and find out how much owners throughout history paid for that house. The owner you are most interested in is the current one, the owner selling the house right now.

Liens and mortgages are also recorded at the courthouse. You can find out whether the current owner has a mortgage on the property; if so, with a little guessing, you can estimate that mortgage's current balance. For example, if the owner bought the house with a thirty-year mortgage two years ago, you know that very little of the house is paid for. If the current owner paid less for the house than he or she is asking, you know the owner wants a profit (although owners do not always get profits).

If a mortgage is still on the house, the owner probably will not be willing to go below the balance of the mortgage. For instance, if an owner still owes $28,500 on the house, he or she will be very reluctant to sell the house for under $28,500. If there is a mortgage, check to see whether it is assumable. If so, it would be very easy for you to step in and continue the payments.

It is common to ask the seller for the current loan balance on the house. Sellers will not always tell you the balance, but many will. Sellers rarely accept offers below their mortgage balances, since they would have to pay money to release themselves from the mortgage. In depressed times, distressed sellers have had to take less for the home than they owed on the mortgage, or they would not be selling the property.

Whatever you find out at the courthouse is information you can use to make a better offer. The first time you visit the courthouse for land information, ask one of the clerks for help. As long as you are courteous and do not hurry the clerk, he or she will be happy to assist you. Many courthouses now have computerized property records, so that you can search for the information yourself at a computer terminal. Even if you are computer illiterate, finding property information often requires just typing an address and you are on your way.

If the seller accepts your offer or if you and the seller agree on a counteroffer, you should hire an attorney to check the house abstract to make sure the title is not *cloudy*. A cloudy title means that the owner does not own the property outright, but that the property is legally tied up in a custody battle or lien of some kind. The seller's attorneys can usually clear up a cloudy title, but make sure you can get a clear title before pursuing the house any further.

Do not buy a house *on contract*. That means that the seller retains the house title until you pay off the house in full. There are many problems with this approach; there is even a chance that you could pay many years on the house and still not own it at the end. Often, sellers will be easier to bargain with if they sell the house on contract. But pass it up, no matter how good the deal is, if the seller refuses to sell other than on contract. When you buy a house, be sure that you can get *full title and deed* to the house when you purchase it. Your attorney can tell you whether this is possible.

THE CURRENT STATUS OF THE PROPERTY

Wise investors are able to quickly size up a seller's situation. From a newspaper advertisement, it is not always easy to see why a house is being sold. The seller's reason for selling is important information that you can use to determine the lowest price possible. The best way to find out why the house is for sale is to ask.

Sellers who are transferred out of town are more willing to bargain than those staying in town. They need to get out from under their current mortgage because they will soon have to start payments on their new one.

Almost without exception, real estate agents get a commission (usually around seven percent) on every house they sell. In many cases, they work hard and deserve their commissions. However, if an agent is involved in the property you are interested in, you automatically know the house must sell for more than the owner wants. Both the owner and the agent must make their money from the sale. Therefore, houses for sale by owner are almost always better deals than those commissioned through agents.

Another thing to remember about real estate agents: They work for the *seller* and not for you, the buyer. Although your money pays the agent's commission, the agent is solely responsible, by law, to be loyal only to the seller. The agent is required to disclose certain facts about the home to you, including flood insurance requirements and special problems such as fresh termite damage. Nevertheless, the agent is not yours and you must treat the agent with caution when discussing too much of your buying plan of attack.

The vacancy of the house is critical also. If the sellers still live in the house, they are not as desperate to sell it as those who are already in their next house. The longer that sellers sit with an empty house, the more eager they are to sell it, the less profit they expect, and the more in control you the buyer will be.

The longer a house is vacant, the lower is its price.

With a *corporate-owned* house, one owned by a business, you sometimes have a little more bargaining power. Maybe an employee was transferred to another city and the employee's company bought the home to expedite the employee's move to the new location. Sometimes, banks own homes (they may have foreclosed on a property and want to sell it for the remaining loan balance).

Corporations and banks generally do not want to be in the real estate business. They want to get rid of any properties in their inventory so they can get on to the business they do best. Therefore, you sometimes have a little more bargaining power when buying corporate-owned homes; the sellers (the corporation) are more willing and able to sustain a loss on the sale than an individual seller might be.

The Condition of the Home

The kind of homes that investors prefer generally would not be owner-occupied or agent-sold homes. Generally, good investors are interested in rental houses that have *not* been lived in for at least a year. Either the house could not sell or it was so physically run-down that real estate agents did not want to take on the selling responsibility for such a small return. Or maybe, for whatever reason, the owner was simply not in a hurry to get rid of the house.

As discussed in Chapter 9, you want a house that is structurally sound, in good physical shape outside, looks terrible both inside and out, and is located in a clean, safe, owner-occupied neighborhood. Buy the worst-looking house on the block and turn it into the best-looking one. This philosophy works extremely well and makes more sense than just about any other rental advice you can get. You want houses that are cosmetically ugly.

The inside should be worse than the outside.

Although not always the case, you can usually fix up the inside of a house much cheaper than the outside. The inside walls and ceilings may have holes in them, the electricity and plumbing may be in terrible shape, the appliances may be ripped out; still, Sheetrock, paint, and carpet are relatively easy and inexpensive to replace.

If the home's wiring and plumbing are in bad shape, most buyers stay away from the house. Bad plumbing and electrical wiring lower the selling price tremendously; yet, wiring and plumbing are not extremely expensive to have done considering your long-term investment. As a matter of fact, the biggest problem your rental house can have is with the wiring and plumbing. Take care of these problems at the start. Expect to replace as much or all of the wiring and plumbing as possible in order to get it in shape for the next twenty years.

Most areas require that licensed electricians and licensed plumbers do all the wiring and plumbing work on a house. In many areas, you the owner are not allowed to work on your own home's wiring unless you are licensed. Hiring licensed personnel is expensive, and these two expenses will be the costliest part of the home's renovation. Think about the savings in the future, however. Good wiring will not cause fires, good plumbing will not cause water damage, and you and your tenants will sleep better knowing that these important parts of the home are in perfect order.

Since you will do most of the remaining renovations yourself or with low-cost hourly employees (see the next chapter for more information on home renovation), you can afford to get the most important factors, wiring and plumbing, taken care of properly.

Brand-new, no-frills, generic white appliances are very inexpensive. Instead of messing with a ten-year-old stove that works half the time, invest in a new one. A new stove, oven, and refrigerator look nice and you will know their history. If the house you buy has old appliances that look suspect, replace them when you renovate to give you years of maintenance-free landlording.

In almost every case, houses with termite damage sell for a much bigger discount than the damage costs to fix.

Today, termite damage is relatively easy to fix. Contrary to popular belief, termites damage houses very slowly. It takes a long time for termites to infest a house so terribly that the house is not structurally sound. A few years ago, the government banned the use of chlordane, an extremely effective termite treatment. There is talk of allowing its use again because it is so effective. However, even without chlordane, pest control services are skilled at ridding most properties of termites.

Houses with active termite damage are extremely difficult to sell. Most buyers want to stay completely away from them. If the house you are considering has termite damage, ask a licensed pest control agent to give you a bid on getting rid of the termites. Many pest control services also fix any wood damage caused by termites. You might be surprised at how cheaply the pest control service can get rid of the problem.

Houses that sell with *structural damage* rarely have damage beyond repair. Sellers are required by law to disclose problems like structural damage. In many cases, structural damage is nothing more than a brick wall that is loose or a floor that sags. But the term *structural damage* automatically scares buyers away from houses, thereby lowering the price considerably. Most of the time, you can easily repair structurally damaged houses with very little expense. If you feel that the damage might be costly, ask a framing carpenter to look at the problem. Generally, framing carpenters can shore up sinking timbers in a matter of minutes.

The Type of Property

Throughout most of the country, it makes sense for investors to buy freestanding, three-bedroom houses. Such homes easily compete with apartment buildings, if bought for a good price. But there are parts of the country where this type of home is not practical. For instance, in New York City high-rise and brownstone apartments take precedence over freestanding houses.

Try to find homes with a garage or at least a carport. Nobody likes to leave their automobile out in the elements. A garage also gives tenants a place to store their lawn and garden equipment.

Keep your eyes open for other types of housing in your area. As mentioned in the last chapter, duplexes and four-plexes are a landlord's dream, since they rarely cost twice or four times as much as single-family houses but they return two to four times the rent. You may miss these jewels when scouring your paper for low-priced homes, since they will be priced slightly higher than single-family homes. Therefore, once you select the five lowest priced houses, read through the rest of the ads to make sure you did not miss a multifamily building.

Two-bedroom houses generally sell for much less than comparable three-bedroom houses. Buyers often shy away from two-bedroom homes since they are difficult to resell. However, wise investors know the rental value of a two-bedroom house. Investors are interested in a house's rental appeal, not its future selling price. Two-bedroom homes compete wonderfully well with one- and two-bedroom apartments. They offer many advantages (such as a yard, garage, and privacy) over apartments, so renters seek them out first.

Two-bedroom homes are hard to sell but easy to rent.

In some areas, mobile homes are attractive rental investments since they offer better depreciation than houses and are very inexpensive to fix up. However, mobile homes do not last as long as permanent homes. In some areas of the country, a two- or three-bedroom mobile home commands as much rental income as a house and is much cheaper to maintain (but you must find a place to put it, with utility hookups; often, you must pay a small fee to park it, if you can't put it on property you own).

Condominiums and cooperatives sometimes make good rental buys, but their appeal has waned since the early 1980s. Remember that they almost all have association dues, which are subject to change and will always rise if they change at all. Some have rental restrictions. Generally, their resale value has not been historically as strong as that of the single-family home or duplex, although resale value is a secondary consideration to you.

Location

You already know to buy homes in good neighborhoods. Nobody wants to rent a house in an unsafe neighborhood. Your competitors have plenty of houses in nice places.

Besides the neighborhood, you must also consider how far you want the rental property to be from your own home. If you buy the house next door, you may see your tenants more often than desired. Buying a home too far from your own also causes problems. Long-distance landlording can be a headache. Most landlords who live farther than fifty to seventy-five miles from their rental property eventually hire a service to take care of the property and to find tenants. As soon as a rental service takes over, you lose profits and control, the two most important parts of successful landlording.

Sometimes, buying homes in small towns that surround yours makes sense.

A good strategy for some landlords who live in large cities is to buy rental property in the surrounding smaller towns. Your rentals will be close enough for you to handle all problems but far enough away so your tenants do not bother you with petty requests. In addition, you will not be competing with your larger town's apartment complexes, and taxes are generally lower in smaller towns.

Moving a House

Never overlook the possibility of moving a good home to a good vacant lot. Many areas of your town are being demolished for new construction; you can buy homes for the cost of demolition and have them moved inexpensively (from two thousand to five thousand dollars, depending on the size of the house, its location, and structure). If you find a great deal on a nice home in a poor area, consider moving it to a better one.

The biggest key to moving a house is finding a vacant lot. There are more good lots than you might realize, and you would be surprised at the number of vacant lots in good housing tracts. Houses burn down and the owners often choose not to rebuild at the same location. By moving your home onto such a lot, you'll make the neighborhood happy, increase tax revenue for the city, and put more rental income in your pocket than if you had bought an existing home in the same neighborhood.

The amount of money you make during your landlording career greatly depends on how much you pay for your houses. Buying and moving a home to a good neighborhood is almost always more cost-effective than buying an existing one in a good neighborhood.

Building movers know how to move homes and keep them intact during the move. Houses require very little work to prepare before moving, and the moving company can do the work for you. Talk with the movers to determine how much they will do and how much you will do. A straight lift-and-move job is a lot cheaper than having the movers also get the house back to its original condition, once it's in place. Ask the movers what the house will need, once it is moved, to prepare it for living. You may be able to do all the work yourself (sometimes, only painting is needed, depending on the condition of the house before the move).

You would be surprised at how well houses can be moved and still remain intact. Some home movers actually recommend keeping the furniture in place when moving an existing house and family, instead of taking the furniture out before the move and putting it back in afterwards. Structural damage rarely occurs with movers who know their job. There are many homes in the country that have been moved and did not even need a touch-up paint job.

Ways to Buy

Your newspaper's "For Sale" columns are not the only places to look for good rental deals. Let your friends know that you are always interested in good bargains. If you have a good relationship with a banker, ask the banker about any foreclosed properties that the bank holds. Many times, banks are willing to let houses go for very little money, simply to get rid of them.

Banks are not the only institutions that foreclose on properties. Savings and loans have many more properties than they care to admit. Mortgage lenders may also be able to direct you to a deal.

The government always has more houses than it ever wants.

Ask at your county courthouse about home auctions and tax sales. If you go three years without paying your property taxes, guess what happens to your property? The government steps in and takes it from you. Of course, this won't happen to you, but it does happen every day to thousands of other people around the country. Usually, these government-foreclosed properties do not have families in them; rather, they are homes that have been abandoned because of divorce, death, or other reasons.

In many instances, the government will sell its inventory of houses for the back-taxes due. Very few people take advantage of this situation. Although some legal work is involved, and buying a house for back taxes is not always a straightforward process, isn't a $750 house worth a little effort? Ask your county courthouse clerks for more information about these homes.

The government often holds auctions for tax-sale houses. To get in on an auction, you only have to know its time and location. Many times, *nobody* shows up at these auctions, so be sure to ask your county clerk's office about them.

Many states around the country have government-run house-selling services for houses that were abandoned or seized. Housing and Urban Development (HUD) and Veterans Administration (VA) are two offices that regularly sell homes below market value.

Summary

Let's say you have followed this book's suggestions so far. You have streamlined your rental properties to the point where they practically take care of themselves, you have quality tenants, and your landlording business is on autopilot. What is your next step? *Buy more properties.*

Empires are made one step at a time, and twenty-five rental properties, properly managed, are not a lot more time-consuming than two or three. The bulk of your time will be devoted to fixing up the property so you can move good tenants in.

With more properties, the odds are greater that you'll have a vacancy—but with more properties, the vacancy's loss of rent is covered by rents from the rest. By now, the risk of more vacancies should not concern you, especially since the open-house approach makes vacancies easy to fill.

This chapter discussed the types of homes to look for, the neighborhoods to look in, and how to find good deals. There are great deals all around you. You only have to find them. Nobody seems to want to get into the rental business when housing is in a bad slump, but that is the *only* time to buy! Buy when nobody else seems interested because that is when prices are lowest.

The importance of buying several low-cost houses instead of one or two higher priced homes cannot be stressed enough. To be successful in the landlording business, your rental return is the primary consideration. Buy your houses right—that is, *cheaply*—and you will compete successfully in the rental property business.

CHAPTER ELEVEN

Renovating Your Rental Properties

RENOVATING RENTAL PROPERTIES does not have to be expensive or extremely time-consuming. You should spend the majority of your time on preparing the house for renting. As the previous chapter discussed, smart land-lords buy rental properties that are run-down, that look awful cosmetically, and that reside in good neighbor-hoods. Getting the home looking its best on the outside often takes a good coat of paint, some shingles and shut-ters, and a thorough yeard clean-up. The inside of the house should feel like new once you're done with it. Fresh paint, new wallboard where needed, new (but generic and no-frills) appliances, and go-with-everything carpet spruce up the inside like you would not believe.

This chapter gives the owner of a newly purchased rental house some tips and ideas for turning that shack into a renter's dream. Renters do not expect palaces. They only expect and deserve an attractive, cozy, clean, safe home that they can be proud of. Chapter 2 explained how inexpensive extras such as ceiling fans, miniblinds, and outside shutters add elegant but inexpensive touches to rental houses that attract good tenants. Attempt to maintain a clean and fresh look and care about tenants' needs, without becoming too extravagant in your spending. Simplicity and uniformity are the keys to keeping more than one rental property maintained and in tip-top shape.

Home renovations are easy. If you never thought you could hammer Sheetrock, you've never watched someone else do it. You take a hammer and pound in the nails and that's about it. The sanding and painting take time, but again, anybody can do the work. This chapter cannot possibly give you an in-depth tutorial on home renovation. The details require many more pages and are better left to the books and television shows completely dedicated to the subject. (An extremely well-written book for home remodeling is Dan Lieberman and Paul Hoffman's *Renovating Your Home for Maximum Profit*.)

Instead of teaching you how to use a hammer, this chapter focuses on helping you determine a rental property's needs. Every home renovation is different because every home is in a different state of disrepair. After reading this chapter, you will know which renovations are necessary, which are not, and which cost little but add lots of rental appeal.

Keep Things Simple and Uniform

The best renovating advice you can have as a landlord is to keep things simple and uniform. Do not paint the walls a different color in every room of the house. Choose a neutral color and stick with it. If you want to break the monotony, paint the kitchen and bathrooms a different color from the rest of the house (these rooms require a different kind of paint anyway, if you want to keep steam from peeling the paint). Flat paint does not last very long on rental property walls. Stick to a semigloss for a longer lasting paint that is also easier to clean.

If you have more than one rental house, use the same colors on *all* your houses. This single tip will save you a lot of time and effort over your landlording career. Actually, the home you live in can be a guide to the color schemes you use on your rental properties. If your taste in color is not too extravagant, paint the outside of your rentals the same color as your own home, so you will always be able to match the paint whenever you need to touch up something. You are more likely to have the right color in your garage and you might get bulk discount rates from your local paint store.

Make your rental homes mirror images of each other.

Sticking with the same color scheme lets you save in other ways as well. You can then use the same shutters, carpet, fixtures, and everything else. Once your houses match, it's easy to replace broken or worn items (you can keep on hand spare shutters, light fixtures, and carpet squares for patching holes).

KEEP COLORS NEUTRAL

Keeping colors neutral does not mean they have to be dull. But if you paint every room in a rental white, your tenants will tire of the walls quickly, and the walls will show dirt faster than if they were another color. Instead of white, paint the walls a light cream color. This color will never go out of style and any furniture your tenants own will fit right in.

If you do not mind spending a little more time, paint the baseboards and all the trim, inside and out, a lighter color than the walls. White works well. This "colonial-style" approach adds an expensive look to any house. Never paint trim or baseboards a darker color than the rest of the walls. This tends to box rooms and makes the house seem smaller. When painting an already dark trim a lighter color, you may have to first apply a primer coat of white paint. Dark colors are difficult to cover otherwise.

Many homes built in the last twenty-five years have no ceiling molding. If yours doesn't have trim, install some. A small trim around the ceiling, painted white, adds an elegant but inexpensive touch to any room. Ceiling trim is a one-time, inexpensive outlay that produces good-looking results forever.

The paler the color, the better it suits various tenants.

When choosing colors, pick pale ones. Virtually any color works, all through a house, as long as it's light enough to accent the house's furnishings. The color of the walls should be unobtrusive so that tenants' pictures and furniture stand out. You can paint the walls yellow or eggshell blue as long as the paint is pale enough to stay in the background.

WAINSCOT LIVING AREAS

An inexpensive trick that really impresses tenants is wainscoting, which is the process of paneling the lower half of the walls and painting the upper half. Cap the joint between the paneling and the painted wall with a thin wood trim painted the same color as the wall. When would-be tenants walk into a wainscoted living room during open house, they will be greeted with a rich-looking living area instead of the stark plasterboard walls they saw at your competitor's place.

Wainscoting is easy and requires only inexpensive paneling. Since the paneling only goes up half the wall, you need to buy only half as much as the room would need for a complete paneling job. The paneling has the added advantage of protecting the walls as well. When a tenant scoots a chair too close to the wall, paneling can absorb the scrape better than painted wallboard.

Between tenant occupancies, wainscoted walls require less maintenance as well. Often, a little furniture polish brightens the paneling's shine. Since the paneling took most of the dents and scuffs of the former tenants, you do not need to repaint the room as often. Many times, touch-up paint here and there is all that is needed.

Think About the Future

Every renovating decision you make should be with long-term ownership in mind. Assume that you will keep this rental house for the rest of your life. This will help you make wiser decisions.

For instance, if the plumbing and wiring need replacing, do it. The last chapter described how an initial investment in wiring and plumbing saves you lots of headaches over the years and also pays off in safety as well. Replace shingles if they appear loose. It is a lot cheaper to do so now than to fix a leaky roof later.

Do not paint a room one crazy color just because you had some leftover paint. Someday, that room will need repainting, and you will have to start all over, because you'll never be able to match the first color. When you wainscot a room, buy an extra piece of paneling and store it in the attic. Later, when a section of paneling needs to be replaced, you won't have to settle for a "close match," as many landlords would.

Doorstops and wallpaper guards pay for themselves over and over.

Put doorstops on every wall on which a door opens. A doorstop is a lot cheaper and easier to install than fixing a hole in the wall later. As you walk through the home, consider every little thing you can do now to stop the big problems from happening in the future. Your landlording career is a long one and you can make it hard or easy.

If the house has wallpaper, install clear plastic wall guards on every exposed corner. Corners never seem to like wallpaper and the wall guard will keep the paper glued down, even if tenants rub against the corner every time they pass it.

WALLPAPER

Wallpaper is an attractive addition to a rental house, but many landlords do not install it because of the time and expense. However, if you know how to hang paper and enjoy the work, by all means add this extra touch. Do not paper all the rooms — walls that look "too busy" get old fast. Only put wallpaper in the kitchen and bathrooms, and be sure to get paper that is water- and steam-resistant.

Papering the walls of a rental property certainly has its drawbacks, so weigh the advantages before you hang the paper. Do not feel that you need to do it. Smooth, well-painted walls look just fine. Some people mistakenly believe that wallpaper covers up a lot of ills, but they are wrong — wallpaper *accents* problems. If your wall has holes or loose Sheetrock or cracks, fix them. The walls must be smooth before putting up wallpaper.

If you do wallpaper, you must first remove any old paper and then you must *size* the walls. Sizing prepares the wall for paper and makes the paper a little easier to remove later, because wallpaper is often difficult to remove. Someday, you will have to remove the paper, so taking the time to size the walls now means tremendously less scraping down the road.

A nice touch that even nonwallpapering landlords can do is to put a wallpaper border around the ceiling of a painted wall. Even the highest quality borders are very inexpensive and most are preglued; with a little water, you will have them up in no time. Wallpaper borders are another example of that extra touch that caring landlords can add to turn a house into a home, and yet, the paper costs little and is easy to install.

Wallpaper borders are much easier to hang and take down than full wallpaper but add almost as much decorative appeal.

SAFETY *ALWAYS* FIRST

Never skimp on safety. Install handrails on the stairs, safety bars in the tubs, and smoke alarms on each floor. If safety is not your number one priority, do not become a landlord; someday, an inadequate wiring job will cause you much grief.

Minimize possible damage and make sure tenants are safe.

During renovation, think about ways to minimize damage. A plumber can add water shutoff valves below each sink, tub, and toilet, to save you lots of water-damage repair bills later. When a sink begins to overflow, your tenant only has to turn off the shutoff valve to stop the water. Once the water is off, there is plenty of time to fix the overflow.

The alternative to individual shutoff valves is to show the tenants where the main water shutoff valve is.

Located outside, it requires a key to access and to shut off. But even if you give your tenants a key, the water will overflow and damage your carpet and any first-floor ceilings long before tenants get the water turned off.

Make sure the house is wired with ample electricity. Two hundred amp service is the least you should have these days and three hundred amp is best. Otherwise, tenants' hair dryers and large televisions will trip the circuits too often. Even if the house wiring is adequate, replace any fuse boxes with circuit breaker boxes. When a circuit trips, your tenant will easily be able to turn the electrical service back on instead of searching for a fuse. Label each circuit clearly so the tenant can find the right circuit without having to try them all.

At your local radio and electrical supply store, you can purchase an electrical outlet tester for a few dollars. These testers have red and green lights that tell you whether an outlet is wired properly. Most important, they warn you when an outlet is not properly grounded (the ground is the third prong on many electrical plugs). If one or more outlets have problems, get an electrician to fix them. This is another safety-first expense that you should never have to repeat.

Consider Your Tenants' Needs

Every time you walk through the house, think about the needs of the people living there. What would you need in each room if you lived there? Tenants want and deserve any conveniences you can give them. Landlords who plan for the long term consider the tenants' needs first, knowing that small investments up front reap large dividends in the future.

Make sure the kitchen has plenty of cabinet space for the home's size. If the bedroom closets are small, consider installing extra shelves at the top for more storage. You want to keep tenants as long as possible. Installing adequate storage pays off. Every time your tenants put dishes away in a kitchen without ample storage space, they will want to move.

Extra phone jacks are extremely easy to install. They don't carry harmful electricity, so you don't need an electrician's license to wire them. A trip to your local phone supply store will produce all the tools, outlets, and wiring you need. Most phone wiring parts come with hookup instructions. You only need to extend and connect two wires (the red and green ones—just remember Christmas colors) from any existing phone outlet in the house to the new ones.

Make sure the master bedroom has a phone outlet. Since these outlets are so easy to install, consider putting them in each bedroom, in the kitchen, and in the living room. If your tenants have the phone company put in extra outlets, the cost is extremely high.

If the house is wired for cable television, make sure there are outlets in places where tenants need them. Most cable television companies are not as lenient as the phone company regarding extra outlets. You may have to pay the company a one-time charge to install an extra outlet. Although tenants will not need as many television outlets as phone outlets, one in the master bedroom would be a special treat. If your tenants want more than two cable television outlets, tell them they will have to foot the bill themselves.

Check every light bulb and replace the dead ones. Once your tenants move in, it's their responsibility to replace bulbs that burn out, but every bulb in the house should be working at the outset.

Install deadbolt locks on all outside doors and make sure all windows lock from the inside. Get a locksmith to key the deadbolts to the same key as the front and back doors. One key per house makes it much easier for you and your tenants to keep track of keys. Make sure every door opens easily. If a door drags on the floor, a hinge is usually loose. Tighten all hinges. Because door hinges are notorious for stripping their screws, you may have to re-move the screws and fill their holes with wood filler before tightening them again. If tightening the hinges does not stop the sagging, plane the bottom of the door so it no longer drags.

For added security, buy an inexpensive peephole for the front door. You can install it in five minutes with a drill. Tenants will appreciate being able to see who is at their front door before they open it.

Make sure the kitchen and bathrooms have adequate towel bars and paper holders. Sometimes, it is difficult to remember these little extras when you are not living in the home. But without them—without adequate storage space, outlets, and towel racks—your tenants will have a difficult time living in your rental for a long period of time. They will never notice the extras when they have them, but they will surely miss them when they do not.

When you install towel bars, shelves, or anything else on the walls, be sure to secure the screws into the wooden *studs* in the walls. Studs are the wood beams that frame the walls. If you have ever seen a house in mid-construction, you have seen the web of wooden studs that forms the basis of the walls. Purchase an inexpensive stud finder at your local radio and electrical supply store to help you find wall studs.

When you first renovate the house, install enough insulation in the walls and attic to keep the home well guarded from the outside elements. Insulation is not ex-pensive, and it saves your tenants lots of money on their utility bills, leaving more money for your tenants and therefore more money for the rent. Weather stripping around all outside doors is also a must, especially for cold-winter areas.

The electrical outlets and switches in the outside walls lose lots of heating and cooling energy. Most home supply stores now sell small packages of insulation al-ready cut to fit electrical outlets and light switch covers. A packet of ten or twenty insulating pads only costs a few dollars, but the pads efficiently fill in the holes in the outside walls.

While insulating the outlets and switches, consider replacing all the switch plates and outlet covers in the house. Over the years, these get painted and papered over so much that they look cheap and old. Switch and outlet plates are extremely inexpensive and their neat and uniform look adds even more to a freshly renovated home.

More landlords are moving away from gas water heaters to electrical ones, even though electric heat is more costly. Heating water is one of the few places a landlord might want to put his or her cost before the tenant's. Every year, more restrictions are placed on gas water heaters. They must be enclosed and properly ventilated, sometimes requiring two or three ducts several inches thick. When you replace a water heater, look at the electric ones instead of going straight for the gas.

Electric water heaters require much less ventilation, cost less, are much easier to install, and are safer than gas heaters. All these factors add up. To lower the tenant's electric bill, put an insulating blanket around the water heater. These blankets are inexpensive at most home improvement stores and pay for themselves the first year. Water heater blankets are a good investment for both gas and electric water heaters.

Eliminate all pests while the house is vacant.

Spraying for bugs in a vacant house is much easier, usually cheaper, and much more successful than after tenants move in with their furniture. Call an exterminator to thoroughly spray the house, attic, and crawl spaces, both inside and out. No tenant likes to see bugs the first day in a new house. Get rid of pests now, completely, and the house will have fewer troubles with insects later.

Bathrooms and Kitchens

Cleanliness is nowhere as important as in these two rooms. Get rid of stains, smells, and mildew. If you buy a house with cracked porcelain, replace it. Quality counts when replacing fixtures. Do not buy the latest style; instead, buy traditional fixtures that will hold up with heavy use. Install the *positive stop* faucets that turn completely off at a fixed point instead of tightening down until the water cuts off. Positive stop faucets save you lots of time in washer replacements and save your tenants money from dripping water costs.

Sometimes white porcelain gets chipped. When this happens, there is little you can do. If the damage is small, ignore it; otherwise, replace the entire fixture. Do not recoat the porcelain. The second coat will chip even easier than the first and you will be out money and time.

Use latex paint on the bathroom and kitchen ceilings. A thin coat is better than a thick one; the thick coat will peel easier than a thin one since moisture condenses easily on bathroom and kitchen walls. In the bathroom, consider installing an exhaust fan that vents upwards through the roof. Make sure the fan is connected to the light switch so it always comes on when someone enters the bathroom (make sure you get a quiet fan; most modern ones are). The fan will help eliminate odors, but more important, it will carry steam out of the bathroom and away from the paint, plaster, and Sheetrock.

Caulking is one of the landlord's best friends. Caulk around all sinks, tubs, toilets, windows, and floors. Nowhere is caulking more important than in the bathrooms. Water damages houses very quickly. Even the best tenants get water on the floors and walls. The last thing you need is water running behind a tub or into floorboard, causing wood rot and inviting termites. Caulking ahead of time saves you lots of time, money, and effort in the long run.

Be sure to use twenty-five–year caulking. It is slightly more expensive (about thirty percent more) than the cheaper caulking but lasts much longer and applies more smoothly. Almost all white caulking can be painted. Use indoor/ outdoor caulking instead of worrying about different kinds for inside and outside. Do not be afraid to use a case or two of caulking when you first renovate your home. The bathrooms and kitchen need a lot. Also, use ample caulking around all outside windows to insulate them well.

Use high-quality, indoor/outdoor caulking.

If the shower has doors, consider replacing them with a rod and a shower curtain. Not all showers work with only a curtain, but many do, especially tub-shower combinations. The shower doors get very dirty and are extremely difficult to clean. They often crack, need lots of caulking, and are generally a pain. You can buy a shower curtain at discount stores for a few dollars. Put up a fresh curtain before each tenant moves in.

If the bathtub has old decals on its bottom, you can remove them by first applying a heat gun or hair dryer to soften their adhesive. Once the adhesive softens, you will be able to peel or scrape the decals off. Be sure you do not scratch the tub surface; a plastic car-windshield scraper works nicely. Whatever adhesive residue remains can be taken up with fingernail polish remover or paint thinner.

Carpeting

When renovating the house, install the carpet last, only after you are through painting and drilling and have moved the appliances in. If you are replacing old carpet, leave it down until you are ready to install the new carpet. The old carpet can catch all the sawdust, loose nails, and paint scrapes; you will then remove all this debris when you remove the carpet. Never install carpet in the bathrooms or kitchen. Spills can easily ruin a carpet; in these rooms, uncovered floors make clean-ups easy.

Make sure you buy a neutral-colored carpet that does not show dirt easily. Stay away from sculptured carpet. Choose a traditional carpet with average-height nap that is easy to clean and looks good.

You might be surprised at how cheaply you can buy carpet. Go to several different carpet supply stores and check price tags before you look at the carpet's color and texture. Most of the home improvement stores sell generic carpet these days, at very competitive rates. Be sure to measure how much you will need before shopping for estimates. Although most stores quote a price per square yard, many will discount further when you buy several rooms' worth.

Do not be afraid of letting the store know that you are a landlord and will do business with them in the future if they will give you a good price. It's a good idea to deal with the manager for the best price.

Wise landlords know that good carpet padding is even more important than good carpet. A good carpet will not last very long without adequate padding. In fact, a good padding under an average carpet makes that carpet feel like the top of the line and also makes it last for a long time. Buy padding when you buy carpet. When cutting extremely good carpet deals, many companies offer to throw in padding free of charge. But it may be better in the long run to pay a few cents more per yard for the higher grade padding than taking the free padding.

The first time you install carpet, hire someone who knows what to do and offer your help so you will learn how it is done. Carpet is not difficult to lay, but it must be stretched properly onto tacking strips. Once you watch and help someone else lay it, you should be able to do it yourself the next time. Laying carpet almost always requires two people because it is difficult to stretch it by yourself. You also need several special tools: A *knee kicker* stretches the carpet as you crawl across it. A carpet that is not properly stretched wrinkles and wears out quickly. A *hot glue seamer* glues two pieces of carpet together. But you don't need these tools very often and they are high priced. Most rental supply stores carry all the carpet-laying tools you need, so do not buy your own.

The Outside

The outside of the house gives would-be tenants that vital first impression. The first step in preparing any home is to pick up trash around the yard, to trim trees and shrubs, and to mow the grass. It is not uncommon for low-priced houses to have overgrown lawns, so the odds are good that you will have to do some yard work before starting on the house itself. Clearing away extra growth around the house gives you easier access when painting and repairing the outside.

Tenants like yards but they do not like yard work.

The yard is both the tenants' friend and enemy. Typically, tenants love the freedom and space of a yard. Yards create a better family environment than do tight apartment dwellings. Despite this, tenants dislike yard work. Sometimes, you must nag tenants to get them to mow the yard. Trimming hedges and trees might as well be done by you, since tenants will rarely get around to it.

When cleaning the yard, consider its future upkeep. Keep trees for shade and keep bushes to accent the house, but get rid of all other growth. Too many bushes and unkempt trees make the house look messy. The more trees and bushes you leave, the more work you make for yourself in the future.

Once the yard is clear, you must begin on the house itself. Scrape all loose paint off the wood. Although you do not have to remove all paint before putting on a new coat, make sure to scrape and brush off any loose and peeling paint you find. Old windowsills are notorious for loose paint, so be thorough.

Keep your future paint job lasting longer by repairing all loose gutters and downspouts. Gutters protect a home's foundation, especially those with basements. Clean out the gutters so water flows through them freely. Unfortunately, gutters need cleaning about twice a year (after spring and fall). To make future maintenance easy, install screens to keep leaves and debris from clogging the gutters. Home improvement stores have plenty of gutter screens and they install easily.

Make sure the downspouts point well away from the walls of the house. You can buy some inexpensive concrete splash guards so the water at the bottom of the spouts gets carried even further into the yard and away from the house. Not only do these splash guards help carry water, but they protect the downspout from the havoc of weed-cutting machines.

Once you get the gutters clean and repaired, put a fresh coat of paint on them that matches the trim on the house. The paint helps lengthen the life of the gutters and makes the house look better.

If the house has no guttering, you can save this maintenance work by doing without guttering altogether. Keep in mind, however, that guttering does help protect the paint and foundation, and your tenants may require guttering over the front door so they stay dry while looking for keys. Many guttering installers offer lifetime guarantees, so the money you spend on guttering today will be a lifetime investment.

Make sure that the roof shingles are all in place. Loose or missing shingles will cost lots someday when a heavy rain decides to soak through to your ceiling and your tenants' possessions. Secure any loose shingles with roofing nails (proper roofing nails do not rust). If you have to replace the entire roof, buy the materials and hire the labor instead of calling a commercial roofing company. The last section in this chapter describes how to find reliable roofing help if you know nothing about roof repairs.

If the roof needs lots of repair, check with your city building office to see whether a building permit is required. Many times, a permit is needed when you repair framing beams or change the structure of a roof. In extreme cases, you might have to resort to hiring a licensed roofing contractor.

Step back to take a good look at the windows of your house. They should all be in good shape and look uniform. On most houses that sell for a low price, the windows need a lot of work. Often, they do not close well, offer little insulation, and look terrible from the outside. Work on the windows, chiseling away where needed, so they open and close with relative ease. After scraping them, paint them carefully. You want them to open and close easily without breaking the paint.

Storm windows insulate and look good, too.

Placing storm windows over the regular windows improves the home in several ways. Storm windows give your tenants added security and insulation. Older house windows often let cold air in much too easily. Storm windows also give a uniform look to the front of most houses. Older homes, especially those with wood sashes, often look more modern after you place single- or double-pane storm windows over the old windows. Although tenants have to open the inside window and the storm window every time they want fresh air, the advantages of security, insulation, and looks will make up for the extra little effort. Most storm windows come with their own screens, so your tenants can open the windows without letting insects in. Since the windows on homes vary in size, measure each window on the house and go to a construction supply house for the storm windows.

Aluminum-frame storm windows are very easy to install. Typically, one person holds a window up on the outside of the house while another drills eight screws through the storm window frame into the house's original window frame. Each window takes about four minutes to install. Once you secure the window, put a bead of caulking around its four sides. Be sure to drill two or three seep holes in the bottom frame at windowsill level, so that any water that does get into the window will leak outside.

Storage is important outside as well as inside. If the house has no garage, consider installing a small storage building in the back yard. Tenants can keep their garden tools and barbecue grill in the building. This keeps yard clutter down and protects the tenants' tools. Small storage buildings are relatively inexpensive, but they are a must if your home has no garage.

Make sure the front and back porches have adequate lighting. Outside lights deter burglars and help tenants feel more secure. If the garage is not attached to the house, install a light outside the garage so tenants can see at night.

Add some inexpensive frills to welcome your open-house guests.

Once you've painted and fixed up the yard, gutters, roof, and windows, your rental home should look wonderful. A few little extras, which most landlords would fail to do, can set your newly renovated home apart from the crowd.

Large, freshly painted wooden house numbers over or next to the front door provide a welcoming look. A new mailbox, or even a freshly painted old one, spruces up the front door even more. If the mailbox is out by the street, paint the post and consider planting a few flowers around it. Put stick-on house numbers on the mailbox so the postal carrier and the tenants' guests will have no problem locating the house. (Neither will your open-house guests.)

Clean and sweep the porch well. If drops of paint are evident, clean them up with turpentine. Paint any outside light fixtures and replace damaged ones. Paint the porch light the same color as the house numbers (and the mailbox, if it's attached to the front of the house).

When your open-house guests arrive, their first impression will be that of quality and attention to detail. They will be greeted by a house that says, "Welcome and come on in."

The Landlord's Tool Kit

Most good books on home remodeling and renovation list the tools you need for different jobs. Over the years, you will build a tool collection suitable to regular landlording maintenance jobs. Once your rental home is finished, you need very few tools. But even if you hire out the renovation work, there will be times when you must fix certain things, so be prepared with the right tools.

Begin with the basics. Buy a hammer, a set of screwdrivers and wrenches, a tape measure, a plane, and a saw. You probably already have most of these. Over the years, you will add to this basic set of as needed. Nobody has to be an expert carpenter to hang a new shelf or tighten the hinges on a screen door.

If you have never used a cordless, battery-operated, combination screwdriver and drill, you do not know what you have been missing. Today, master carpenters would rarely leave home without one. Although you can save money initially by buying a hand drill, you'll save so much time over the years using a cordless that it will pay for itself many times over.

The first time you install ten or twelve miniblinds without a cordless drill, you will be convinced that a cordless is the only solution. They save you hours of manual drilling and screwdriver turning. Get a good cordless drill that can hold a charge for thirty minutes to an hour under heavy use. Buy a spare battery pack so you can drill while the spare battery charges.

Get a cordless, combination drill and screwdriver to save hours of time.

This chapter already discussed buying a circuit tester for electrical outlets and an electronic stud finder for the walls. They both pay for themselves in safety and time saved. Without a circuit tester, outlets may be wired incorrectly; without a stud finder, you may have to drill several holes in the walls before finding a wooden stud.

If the house has screens or screen doors, buy a screen repair roller. Most screens that pop out will go right back in. Unless a broken screen is actually ripped, you can usually repair it in a few minutes without spending a dime. To make screen repairs even more infrequent, install a screen guard on every screen door (children and pets are the biggest threat to screen doors). Screen guards are decorative metal bars that help protect screens from hands and feet.

Do not scrimp on tool quality. An old adage says that work is only as good as the tools used. Buy the best tools you can find. Several tool manufacturers offer lifetime warranties, so you'll only have to pay for a particular tool once.

The nice thing about tools is they are usually tax-deductible items and you have to buy them only once. When you renovate your second or third house, you will already have all the tools you need.

Getting Help

Houses are extremely difficult for one person to renovate. Two people can work more than twice the speed as one, so hire help whenever you think you need it. The less "handy" you are, the more you need experienced help. The money you pay hired help is tax deductible, and the sooner you finish the house, the sooner you can rent it. You do not need to hire a professional contractor, only someone who has worked on home renovations in the past. Since the house building/renovation market changes so often, there are always people looking for honest temporary work.

Over your landlording career, you will meet several people who are good at different aspects of home repair and renovation. Keep their names and phone numbers so you can call them when you need someone. A roofer's helper is always a good name to have. Generally, you can buy shingles very cheaply and hire a roofer's helper to put them on, even if it means tearing the old roof completely off first. By putting the labor and supplies together yourself, you save many dollars over what you would spend for a roofing company to do the work.

You will find all the workers you need at your county's local employment agency.

At any one time, there may be several carpenters, electricians, plumbers, roofers, or general repair workers looking for temporary work at your county's local employment office. These workers will be happy to have some work, because their incomes fluctuate with the whims of the local economy. Not only can you usually get any help you need there, but you can make some good contacts with people who can help you in the future as well.

If you just need strong backs to carry, load, and unload materials and to work in the yard, contact colleges in your area. Most have job-finding services for students who need extra money. A college fraternity is also a good place to find many strong hands for a short amount of time and money.

Be courteous and fair to your workers, pay them daily, and buy pizzas for lunch. This way, you will be able to get good help whenever you need it.

Summary

Not good with a hammer? Good, you will have more fun and learn more the first time you renovate a rental property. Besides getting and keeping good tenants, your property's renovation is vital to its long-term maintenance. This chapter presented some common landlording ideas to start you thinking about renovation in the right way.

The key to successful and easy rental maintenance is simplicity and uniformity. Keep your colors neutral and your houses consistent. If you have more than one rental house (which you will have once you are successful with your first one), keep the same styles and paint in all of them. When you need an extra hand, do not hesitate to hire one. It is difficult to renovate a house by yourself, and sometimes impossible, even for home do-it-yourselfers and professionals.

Whatever renovation you do, keep the long term in mind at all times. Invest up front so you reap dividends later. Make sure the wiring and plumbing are in good shape. Scrape old peeling paint away before applying a new coat. Properly stretch carpet and put good padding underneath so it lasts a long time. Add storm windows over old existing windows to improve appearance and insulation. Everything you can do now makes your rental home more attractive to good tenants and keeps them there for a long time.

CHAPTER TWELVE

Record Keeping and Computerizing Your Rental Properties

THESE DAYS, IT seems as if there are two kinds of people: those who love computers and those who curse them. Usually, most people who dislike computers do not understand them and are afraid of them. As a landlord, your record keeping is so simple that you may never need a computer; you only have to keep track of two items: expenses and income. If you have only one or a handful of properties, you can probably do all your record keeping by hand.

Nevertheless, since computers are getting less expensive and easier to use every day, you might consider getting one. Computers can help with word processing and tax preparation, which even one-house landlords can appreciate.

Whether to use a computer or not is up to you. They are nothing more than tools to help you do your work. Just as the typewriter improved the work of scribes many years ago, computers simplify many paperwork tasks. This chapter describes the record keeping needs of landlords and how landlords can integrate computers into their business.

This chapter is no replacement for a good introduction to computers. There are many easy computer books for beginners on the market these days. Once you have decided on the kind of software you want to use with your computer, *DOS 5: Everything You Need to Know* and the Visual Learning Guides from Prima Publishing are among the best books you can buy to get started. If you have never used a computer but feel that one might streamline some of your paperwork, check out these books to learn more about what you can expect.

Landlords and Record Keeping

KEEP *ALL* RECEIPTS

If you do nothing else, *keep all rental property receipts*. Receipts give you an expense trail at tax time and provide proof during an audit. If you have more than one rental house, write the correct house's address on each receipt belonging to that house. If the receipt has no detail, write the store name and a list of the items purchased. In the eyes of the Internal Revenue Service, detailed record keeping is more important than just about anything else you do.

A canceled check is not always enough proof during a tax audit. Receipts support the checks you write.

As Chapter 8 pointed out, a separate checking account for your rental properties shows the IRS that you made a serious effort to separate your business funds from your personal funds. Whether or not you have a separate account, get a receipt for every check you write to help support every penny you deduct. Canceled checks do not make good detailed records and the IRS may want all related receipts to support the checks you write.

Keeping track of receipts is not everyone's idea of fun, but it is a necessary evil. If your record keeping skills are terrible, you can still be a successful landlord; but you *must* keep all your receipts (if only in a shoe box or whatever else is handy) in case you ever have to support the deductions you took at tax time.

GIVE YOUR TENANTS RENT RECEIPTS

Every step you make to show concern for details is another step toward supporting your tax position. If your tenants pay by check, you do not have to write receipts because the tenants' checks will be their receipts. Nevertheless, many landlords purchase cash-received receipt booklets from an office supply store and give their tenants a rent-paid receipt each month.

Not only should you be able to back up your expenses with receipts, but you should be able to back up deposits to your checking account as well. Having a rent-paid receipt for every rent deposit you make not only shows concern for record keeping, but it also gives you a clear payment history, in case you need to recommend a tenant to another landlord some time in the future.

KEEP A CAR LOG

Automobile mileage is a deductible business expense as long as the mileage is directly related to your rental property and as long as you *keep a detailed written log in the car*. The Internal Revenue Service is a stickler about mileage records. Producing a two-year-old, frayed car log showing each mile you drove for rental property business is very important if you get audited. Make an entry every time you go out showing where you went and the miles involved.

Some landlords just guess at mileage, but guessing, no matter how conservative, will rarely hold up at tax time. You might be surprised at how many miles you actually drive. For most people, keeping a log in the car actually improves the mileage reported. It is too easy to fail to record mileage if you have to wait until later. A log in the car is handy and encourages you to record the mileage right after the actual trip.

Keeping an up-to-date car log typically improves the mileage you would otherwise record.

If you drive to collect rent, you can deduct the mileage. If you drive to buy rental house supplies, you can deduct the mileage. If you work on the rental house, show it during open house, or go to the bank to deposit the rent check, you can deduct the mileage. The mileage allowance adds up, so be conscientious about recording it. Each year, the amount of miles you can deduct changes (it usually rises in your favor as auto costs increase). Mileage is an important and legitimate way to offset rental income for tax purposes.

Landlords and Accountants

Rarely does a landlord with only a few properties need the services of an accountant each month. Unless you incorporate, the odds are good that you keep records on a *cash basis* (as opposed to the *accrual basis* required for corporations); that is, you record expenses when they occur and record income when it arrives. A single log (in addition to the car log mentioned in the last section) is all you need, showing the date, description, and amount of each transaction. You need nothing fancy; a simple spiral notebook will do nicely.

At tax time, even one-property landlords should consider using an accountant. The tax laws change too often for you to keep up with them, unless tax work happens to be your specialty. A certified public accountant (CPA), an accountant, or a tax preparer will be able to find deductions where you may not and identify problems before they get out of hand.

The tax code is too complex for most landlords to tackle on their own.

The type of help you procure depends on your confidence in your own work and the amount of money you want to spend. Tax preparers will produce accurate tax returns, but they are limited on the amount of tax-planning advice they can give you. Accountants are more costly, but they can provide tax-planning services; if you have lots of properties, accountants can help you set up an organized record keeping system to ease your tax-time burden. CPAs are even more expensive; they must meet strict educational requirements every year to maintain their certifications; on the whole, they are more up-to-date on changes to the tax laws as they affect your property.

Some landlords like to do all their own record keeping and tax preparation. There is nothing wrong with that, especially for landlords confident in their numerical abilities. A computer can help here, but it can never replace the abilities of a trained accountant or tax preparer. When you hire another person to take over your tax-preparation responsibility, that person can act as an objective party in the event that you are audited. Before accountants put their signature on a tax return, they scrutinize it for errors and possible fraudulent activity. Most accountants take full responsibility for errors they cause and will pay the penalty fees for you if they make a mistake that causes you more tax liability.

In most cases, the fees you pay a tax preparer or accountant are deductible. When you consider how much accountants save you in missed deductions and how much they protect you in case of an audit, hiring them makes a lot of sense, even for the most budget-minded landlord.

Tax preparation time is not the time to save taxes — the year leading up to it is.

The most important time to ask your accountant for tax advice is *before* tax time. The beginning of the tax year is when you should start planning your tax-saving strategies. People often want to lower their taxes at the time they pay them, but by then it is too late. An accountant can provide you with lots of tax-saving help if you ask early enough in the tax year. Start planning your year's taxes on the first of January so you'll pay the least amount of tax possible at the end of the year.

If you have a lot of rental property income, you may be required to file quarterly tax returns. Quarterly tax payments were made more difficult than ever starting in 1992, because each quarter you are required to reevaluate your current financial status for the year. An accountant's help with quarterly payments is almost a requirement these days. If you are required to file quarterly tax payments, you almost certainly will need some help computing their totals.

Landlords and Computers

The computer is not the answer to everything. For the small-time property owner, it could be more of a burden than a help, unless the owner is already familiar with computers. Although computers are cheaper now than ever before, you will end up spending several hundreds and maybe thousands of dollars for a new one with a printer and adequate storage capacity. Read as much as you can about the computers currently on the market before buying one. They differ greatly in prices and capabilities.

Many community colleges offer short courses for new computer users and buyers. You can learn a lot about them in such courses, which usually include hands-on demonstration and helpful advice for those people who say they cannot even spell *PC*. Computers can be easy to use and a lot of fun. Children have known this for several years now, but many adults are slow to realize it.

CHOOSING A COMPUTER

Although there are many different kinds of computers on the market, *microcomputers* (desktop computers, sometimes called "personal computers" or PCs for short) generally fall into one of two broad categories: Apples and their compatibles or IBMs and their compatibles. Apple Corporation is the main source for Apple computers, although several other companies make add-on products. You may have heard of the Apple Macintosh, one of Apple's best-selling home and small-business microcomputers. IBM Corporation is of course the maker of IBM computers, but many other companies make compatibles. An IBM compatible is almost always guaranteed to work exactly like any other IBM compatible.

Despite the impressive technical abilities of Apple computers, IBM PCs and their compatibles strongly dominate the microcomputer market. In the world of computers, it is vital that you own the same type of computer as other people with whom you might want to share files. There are many more *software programs* (the seemingly magical instructions that tell the computer what to do) written for IBMs than for Apples. If you have friends that own Apples, you might consider purchasing an Apple computer. But for most first-time computer buyers who want to use the computer for record keeping, word processing, and tax preparation, IBM compatibles generally offer a wider assortment of programs and capabilities.

Buy your computer from an established business. Many mail order and small computer distributors have gone out of business over the years.

Whatever computer you decide to buy, purchase it from a distributor who has been in business for a while. Over the last few years, there have been many horror stories about computer companies going in and out of business quickly. You do not want to buy a computer from a vendor only to find that nobody is around to help you in six months if something goes wrong. If you buy from an established company, you should have no problem with repairs or add-ons in the future.

WORD PROCESSING

Nothing the computer can do will help you more than *word processing*. Word processing programs turn your computer into a computerized typewriter that makes writing, editing, printing, and changing documents easier than you would ever think possible. Secretaries all over the world are throwing away their typewriters and replacing them with computerized word processors.

Unlike typewriters, nothing you type using a word processor goes to paper until you are completely finished with proofreading and editing. When you use a typewriter, mistakes are very difficult to correct since they appear on paper. Even worse, rearranging paragraphs is almost impossible without scissors and tape, unless you retype the entire document.

Figure 12-1.   *A sample screen from Word for Windows.*

```
 ─                    Microsoft Word - C:\LEASE.DOC                 ▼ ♦
 ⇒  File  Edit  View  Insert  Format  Tools  Table  Window  Help          ♦
 ┌──┬──┬──┬──┬──┬──┬──┬──┬──┬──┬──┬──┬──┬──┬──┬──┬──┬──┬──┬──┐
 │  │  │  │  │  │  │  │  │  │  │  │  │  │  │  │  │  │  │  │  │
 └──┴──┴──┴──┴──┴──┴──┴──┴──┴──┴──┴──┴──┴──┴──┴──┴──┴──┴──┴──┘
                                              (initials) _____

                         * Residence Lease *

      This lease, made and entered into this _____ day of _____, by a
   between _____, of _____, _____, hereina
   called the "landlord," and _____, of _____,
   _____, hereinafter called the "tenant."

      The landlord owns the following described real estate and premises, situa
   _____, County, _____:
   _____

      The landlord rents and leases to the tenant, the above described premises
   the _____ day of _____, for _____ mo

      The tenant promises and agrees to pay the landlord as rental the total su
   _____ payable as follows: _____
   the security/cleaning deposit paid to landlord at the execution of this contr
   entire security/cleaning deposit will be refunded to the tenant within ten (1
   after tenant's normal lease termination or move-out, whichever comes last, if
   property is left in move-in condition and will be escrowed in a safety bank a
   until such time.  The security/cleaning deposit's refundable amount will be p
 ┌────────┬───────┬────────┬───────┬────────┬────────┬──────────┐
 │ Pg 1   │ Sec 1 │  1/ 3  │ At 3" │ Ln 13 Col 1 │ 100%  │   NUM    │
 └────────┴───────┴────────┴───────┴────────┴────────┴──────────┘
```

Figure 12-1 shows a computerized word processing program, *Word for Windows*, in action. The words typed at the keyboard appear on the computer screen, where you can easily change, move, or delete them. Only after correcting any mistakes you see on the screen (by using simple keystrokes), do you print the document to paper. Once on paper, if you still see mistakes, you can correct them again on the computer's screen and print a fresh copy without having to retype the entire document.

Today's word processing programs automatically check spelling and grammar, provide a thesaurus, and offer so many more features that there are literally hundreds of books dedicated solely to word processors on the market today. Despite their power, word processors are extremely easy to use and range in price from twenty dollars to a few hundred dollars. You must purchase the word processing program in addition to the computer hardware to turn your computer into a word processor.

Word processors allow landlords to easily store and retrieve old leases, write new leases, keep correspondence filed by property, and maintain lists of workers' names and phone numbers. A word processor basically acts like a file cabinet for your paperwork as a landlord.

The word processing program is the mainstay of any computerized landlording activity. Usually when a new tenant moves into a house, the new tenant's lease is only slightly different from the previous tenant's. Only the names, amounts, and dates change; the rest of the lease generally stays the same. With a word processor, you can call up the old tenant's lease on the screen, update the information, and print a new lease in a matter of seconds. The old lease is still safely tucked away in the computer's storage (on a *disk*, a platter that stores information and programs in a manner similar to the way an audio tape stores music), and the new lease is always available in case you need it. With the press of a few keys, you can make as many printouts of the lease as you like. With a word processor, every copy is an original.

If you buy a computer strictly for word processing, you will be glad you made the purchase. However, there is a lot more you can get your computer to do.

RECORD KEEPING

Computers are wonderful tools for storing and retrieving information. Managing financial information is a breeze with the computer's calculation capabilities. The computer will keep track of your expenses and income, storing them under any department or budget title you prefer and summing year-to-date totals in an instant.

The problem with computerizing your record keeping is that many landlords may not have enough record keeping needs to warrant the computer's use. Unlike word processing, which helps almost any written task, computing may be overkill for financial record keeping alone.

Consider what happens when you get a rental house key duplicated for $1.25. Is that small amount worth turning on your computer, starting the record keeping program, entering the date, description, and amount, saving the information to the computer's storage, and turning the computer off? Probably not. The truth is that the recording of most expenses and income for many landlords is still best done, even in today's high-tech times, with pen and paper in a journal. Further, if you write a check for most or all of your property-related expenses, you already have a good record of each expense. Entering the expense into the computer becomes a time-consuming duplication of effort.

The more properties you have, the more you need computerized record keeping to keep records and to streamline end-of-the-year tax computations.

As you buy more properties, the computer becomes a much more viable record keeping tool. Keeping a variety of financial records becomes difficult without the filing capabilities of a computer. The more you use your computer and the more you learn about it, the more ways you'll find to improve your daily landlording tasks.

There are lots of programs available that track all your income and expenses; that keep personal and business income and expenses separate; that keep track of bank balances, rental income and expenses, and depreciation; and that maintain tax records. Figure 12-2 shows one such program, *Microsoft Money*, that manages an online computerized checking account. Instead of writing

Figure 12-2.   *A sample screen from Microsoft Money.*

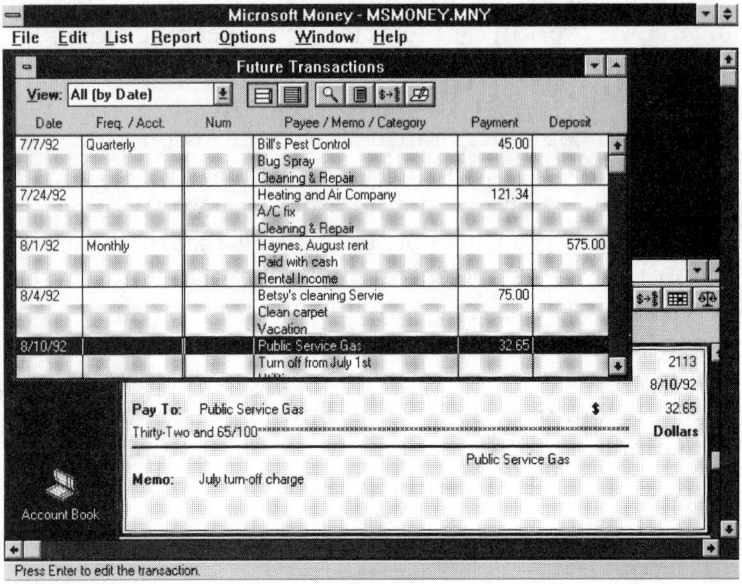

checks by hand and then entering duplicate information into the computer, you can actually issue commands to the computer, so that it prints a check for you while entering and storing all the information in the proper accounts.

Some people do not like to convert their records to the computer's required format. Over the years, these people may have maintained excellent records by hand. After becoming successful landlords, they want to computerize their records but they do not want to change the way they keep track of things. Although a personal and business finance program like Microsoft Money is very flexible, people cannot make it do exactly what they want.

If you are willing to learn a little more about using your computer, you may feel more at ease using an *electronic spreadsheet* program rather than a specific financial record keeping program. An electronic spreadsheet is sometimes called a "word processor for numbers" because

Figure 12-3.   *A sample screen from a landlord's customized Lotus 1-2-3 program.*

```
A:A18: (D1) U [W10]                                                    READY

                              B              C    D      E        F
1              1993 -- 1013 South Illinois Rent House
2                                               Rents
3      Date    Description                    Received  Repairs  Supplies
4      -----------------------------------------------------------------
5   23-Jan-92 Bryson, Jan. rent                $265.00
6   14-Feb-92 Check #2036, phone calls                   3.20
7   27-Feb-92 Bryson, March rent                265.00
8   30-Mar-92 Bryson, April Rent                265.00
9   29-Apr-92 Bryson, May Rent                  265.00
10  29-Apr-92 True Dollar: Door latch bolts                3.20
11  30-Apr-92 Lock Doc: Shed's lock keyed                          22.11
12  23-Apr-92 Blocks and parts to fix porch              51.06
13  07-May-92 Electric House: Alarm battery                        15.23
14  07-May-92 Building Bob's: Window material            30.49
15  05-May-92 Southland's: Tape for window                         1.06
16  01-Jun-92 Bryson, June rent                265.00
17  12-Jun-92 Jack Carner, plumber. #2076                60.00

           A             B              C    D      E        F
500                                   Totals:  $795.00  144.75   38.40
RELOTUS.WK3
```

it allows you to write, manage, and print rows and columns of numbers as easily as a word processor manipulates words. The most popular electronic spreadsheet today is *Lotus 1-2-3*. Figure 12-3 shows a computer screen from a landlord's customized Lotus 1-2-3 program. Notice that instead of a fixed format for the data (as Microsoft Money required), Lotus 1-2-3 is able to display the numbers and descriptions any way the user desires, even duplicating the look of a handwritten journal, if that is what the landlord wants.

Electronic spreadsheets are more flexible than financial programs, but they require a little more learning. Although they are not difficult to use, you must be able to create your own *spreadsheets* (financial record formats). Finance programs such as Microsoft Money are more rigid in the way they present the information, but you have to know less up front to use them. The more you learn about your computer, the more you may want to control the look and feel of your records. You might want to start with a financial program, then switch to a spreadsheet program as your needs and computer knowledge grow.

Whatever route you decide to take with your computerized record keeping, your primary goal should be accuracy. The computer does not make sloppy mistakes. If a computer produces an incorrect result, the odds are extraordinarily high that the person using it typed a wrong total or gave the computer an incorrect instruction. The computer will help you produce more accurate records as long as you carefully enter the amounts into the computerized files.

After accuracy, the primary advantage to computerized record keeping appears at tax time. Depending on how your record keeping system is set up, at the end of the year you may be able to press a button and print out your tax returns or at least print all the information your tax preparer will need to produce an accurate return.

TAX PREPARATION

Setting up the computer so it produces instant tax returns is not always as easy as the computer magazines and dealers might lead you to believe. Nevertheless, it is possible to produce automatic tax return information—as long as you diligently record all income and expenses properly throughout the year and as long as your computer is set up to format the data properly.

If you recently bought a computer and are unsure about where to begin computerizing your property's records, ask your tax preparer for help. Either the tax preparer will be able to recommend appropriate programs or will know someone who can.

Do not expect to have an instant tax return the first year you computerize your property. In fact, there may be cases where it would be better to not get an instant return. No computer is better at spotting tax problems than a trained tax preparer. Your accountant should always review your computerized records. Just because the computer printed it does not mean the information is accurate; you may have made a mistake while entering some of the data.

Your accountant may want you to use a record keeping program that ties directly into his or her own tax preparation program. As the familiar tax return appears on the screen, the accountant directs the program to search the appropriate files for your records. After all the data is entered, the program automatically computes totals, looks up the appropriate taxes, and prints a return.

Letting your accountant produce the final tax return is probably the best solution for most landlords, even those landlords who are themselves computer literate and heavily computerized. You can use your computer for word processing and record keeping throughout the year. When tax time comes around, give your computerized files to your accountant instead of handing over a shoe box full of unorganized receipts (as many noncomputerized landlords might do). From your files, the accountant produces a tax return, after reviewing all the information for accuracy and finding extra deductions where appropriate.

RENTAL PROPERTY PROGRAMS

Some programs were specifically written with the landlord in mind. These track rent expenses, tenant information, property descriptions, income, and expenses. Figure 12-4 shows a sample screen from *Rentman*. Notice that it stores all pertinent rental information. It also keeps track of the year-to-date totals and prints end-of-month and end-of-year reports for you and your tax accountant.

Such programs are wonderful for landlords who don't have the time or interest but still see the need for computerizing the property's records. There are drawbacks, however, to using programs dedicated so much to a single

Figure 12-4. *A sample screen from Rentman.*

```
╔═══════════════════════════════════════════════════════╗
║                   TENANT DATA SCREEN                    ║
║  Name  HAYNES       , DIANA        Building  1   Unit  1║
║        (Last)        (First)                            ║
║  Street Address   1013 S. Illinois   Married ▓  Kids ▓  ║
║  City, State, Zip Miami, FL 41172    Residents ▓        ║
║                                      Pets Not allowed    ║
║  Phone #: (346)555-4905                                 ║
║                                      Rent  450 Security 450║
║  Employer  Totem Enterprises                            ║
║                                      Prepaid Rent      0 ║
║  Street Address   4030 East 57th Place  Delinquent Rent 450║
║  City, State, Zip Miami, FL 41199    Late Charges   0.00 ║
║                                                          ║
║  Work Phone #: (343)555-6444         Total Past Due  450.00║
║                                                          ║
║  Late Chg Type 1 Lvl1 Days 5 Lvl2 Days 10  Moved In  04/01/93║
║  1st Level % 0   1st Level Flat Chg 15  Lease Expires 09/30/93║
║  2nd Level % 0   2nd Level Flat Chg 5                   ║
║                                      Last Rent Incr Amt 0║
║  Notes  Owns 2 cars                  Increase Date  /  / ║
║     ┌────────────────────────────────────────────────┐  ║
║     │ (B)uilding data  (U)nit data  (E)dit  (Q)uit   │  ║
║     └────────────────────────────────────────────────┘  ║
╚═══════════════════════════════════════════════════════╝
```

business; you almost always have to adapt the way you work to the program's requirements. Such programs are rarely flexible enough for you to modify the way the data is stored. Another drawback is that they rarely share data with other programs, a vital consideration at tax time, if your accountant has a tax preparation program that cannot communicate with your program.

Once you buy a computer, there are thousands of programs to help you with your landlording business. For instance, there are many ways that computers can work with numbers. The computer screen in Figure 12-5 shows a program that produces estimates for remodels, *Remodel Estimator*. Before renovating your next house, you can put the home's needs into this program. The program then produces a detailed inventory of the supplies needed along with estimated costs of the complete renovation and any part of it. The program's primary drawback is its timely requirement of pricing information. You must constantly update its built-in inventory prices for building supplies in order for it to give you an accurate estimate. Nevertheless, if you renovate houses often, such a program becomes an asset in producing quick and accurate cost estimates for loan applications and budgeting purposes.

Figure 12-5. *A sample screen from Remodel Estimator.*

COSTCODE	DESCRIPTION	UNIT	TRADE	MANHOUR	COST ($)
030100	SEALER FOR CONCRETE	SF	CONC	1.000	33.250
06	*** WOOD & PLASTICS			0.000	0.000
060504	DRYWALL NAILS,GALVANIZED	LB	CARP	0.000	1.050
060506	COMMON NAILS,ALL SIZES,PLAIN	LB	CARP	0.000	0.640
060508	FINISH NAILS,GALVANIZED	LB	CARP	0.000	0.730
060514	WOOD CONNECTOR PLATE,W/BOLTS	EA	CARP	0.210	20.300
060526	WOOD JOIST HANGERS,2"X4" JOISTS	EA	CARP	0.050	1.900
060551	WOOD SCREWS,#8, 1" LONG	C	CARP	0.000	2.650
061020	POSTS PRESSURE-TREATED,4"X4"	LF	CARP	0.030	1.800
061021	POSTS,PRESSURE-TREATED,6"X6"	LF	CARP	0.040	3.100
061022	DECKING,PRESSURE-TREATED,2"X4"	LF	CARP	0.012	0.680
07.	*** MOISTURE AND THERMAL CONTROL			0.000	0.000
071102	POLYETHYLENE VAPOR BARRIER,0.002" THIC	SQ	JOUR	0.180	5.790
071108	POLYETHYLENE VAPOR BARRIER,.008" THICK	SQ	JOUR	0.250	10.500
08	*** DOORS, WINDOWS & GLASS			0.000	0.000
081110	DOOR,STEEL 24 GA.3'X6'-8",HALF GLASS,C	EA	SPEC	3.000	480.000

Since there are so many good programs available to computer owners, you should shop around and ask a lot of questions before buying any programs. Understand from the start that computer programs are still rapidly evolving. A program you begin using today for your record keeping may be made obsolete by a much better one from a different manufacturer tomorrow. Ask the software seller if you can try the program before you buy it. See if you can borrow a spare program manual for a weekend to read about the program's features. Some programs, such as Rentman and Remodel Estimator, are called *shareware programs*. Although such a program is not free, you can freely try it for a few days to see if you like it well enough to use it. If you decide to keep it, you can send the distributor a check for the cost of the program to register it legally under your name. This way you receive updates to it as they are written.

PROGRAMS MENTIONED HERE

The programs mentioned in this chapter are for illustrative purposes only. There are so many good programs today for a landlord to use that there is no way to give anything other than a small overview of what's available.

Most newsstands now carry computer magazines that describe all the new software introduced each month. For a complete list of current titles, ask at a computer store near you for directions to a good publication that lists programs (there are many lists and catalogs available).

Neither Prima nor the author can endorse someone else's product as being reliable or effective. Nevertheless, if you are interested in more information on the programs mentioned in this chapter, you can write to their companies at the addresses listed below. You are encouraged to look at other titles as well, finding the ones that suit your own needs best.

Word for Windows, Microsoft Money:
Microsoft Corporation
One Microsoft Way
Redmond, WA 98052-9953
800-426-9400

Lotus 1-2-3:
Lotus Corporation
55 Cambridge Parkway
Cambridge, MA 02142
800-223-1662

Rentman:
QuickSoft Management Systems
2404 W. Mangold Ave.
Milwaukee, WI 53221

Remodel Estimator:
CPR, Inc.
P.O. Box 3465
Berkeley, CA 94703
415-654-8338

Summary

Record keeping is a necessary evil for landlords. As far as the IRS is concerned, record keeping is the most important part of your business. Whether you keep your receipts in a shoe box or logged on a computer, receipts and detailed logs provide your back-up and alibi if you ever get audited.

Only you can decide whether you need a computer. Before ruling one out, make sure you have looked at computers, have seen what they can do, and have seen how easy they are to operate. Record keeping alone is not a good enough reason to buy a computer, but word processing and tax preparation programs can save you more time than you might have thought possible. Before using computers, however, you must learn a little about them. Although they are getting less expensive and easier to use all the time, computers are not yet for everybody.

This chapter gave you an overview of some programs that might help you as a landlord. Only a limited survey of programs is possible because there are thousands on the market today. Stop in at your local computer store to see what they have to offer. Be sure to shop at established stores, and trust your tax preparer for advice more than the computer sales clerk. Arm yourself with knowledge before going into the store. The more computer books you read, classes you attend, and knowledge you gain about computers, the more effective you will be with one and the better deal you will make at the computer store.

APPENDIX

Forms for Landlording

Figure 1.   *A sample rental application.*

** Application For Rent **

_____

** PERSONAL INFORMATION **

Name: _____   Social Sec. #: _____

Phone: _____   Address: _____   How long? _____

Landlord: _____   Phone: _____   Rent: $_____

Previous address: _____   Landlord: _____

Phone: _____   Previous rent: $_____   How long? _____

Pets? _____   How many, what kind? _____   Smoker? ___

List names of each person who will live here:

_____

Emergency name and phone: _____

** WORK INFORMATION **

Occupation: _____   Present employer: _____   How long? _____

Gross income: $_____   Supervisor: _____   His/her phone: _____

Previous employer: _____   Supervisor there: _____

Other sources of income: _____

** BANKING INFORMATION **

Savings bank and acct. #: _____   Checking acct. #: _____

Credit card: Type: _____   Acct. #: _____

Credit Reference: Name: _____   Acct. #: _____

** AUTOMOBILE INFORMATION **

Car makes: _____   Models: _____   Years: _____

Financed with: _____

*** The above statements are accurate. By signing this application, I authorize reference disclosure for purposes of leasing the property at the address listed above.

Signature: _____   Date: _____

Note: ID is required when you finish this application. This speeds the process and guards against possible problems later.

Figure 2.   *A residence lease.*

(initials) _____

_____

* Residence Lease *

This lease, made and entered into this _____ day of _____,

by and between _____, of _____,

_____, hereinafter called the "landlord," and

_____, of _____, _____,
hereinafter called the "tenant."

The landlord owns the following described real estate and premises,

situated in _____ County, _____:

_____

The landlord rents and leases to the tenant the above described premises

from the _____ day of _____, for _____ months.

The tenant promises and agrees to pay the landlord as rental the total

sum of _____

payable as follows: _____

_____ for the security/cleaning deposit paid to landlord at the
execution of this contract. The entire security/cleaning deposit will be
refunded to the tenant within ten (10) days after tenant's normal lease
termination or move-out, whichever comes last, if the property is left in
move-in condition and will be escrowed in a safety bank account until such
time. The security/cleaning deposit's refundable amount will be prorated
accordingly if the property is left in less than acceptable condition. The

sum of _____is

already paid for the first full month's rent of occupancy (_____). The

sum of _____
will be payable on the first (1st) day of each and every month of the lease

Figure 2. *(continued)*

(initials) _____

_____

term (_____ full months) until this lease has expired to complete the full sum payable.

No part of said money shall be due and payable until the tenant has been placed in the actual possession of said premises with the keys needed to gain access. This has been done as of the date of this contract.

It is agreed that the tenant will keep and maintain all portions of the building let to him or her by the terms of this contract in as good a state of repair as the same are turned over to tenant. This means woodwork, walls, floors, ceilings, windows, screens, doors, carpet, shades, electric, grounds, plumbing, and outside storage, all of which may be inspected by the landlord on notice from the tenant of intent to vacate and in no event will this lease terminate unless the foregoing is acceptable to the landlord. Normal use without evident mars will not constitute violation.

The tenant agrees to be responsible to pay for the repair of any damage done to any of the buildings or grounds by any of tenant's family or guests. If the tenant notices any signs of property damage or signs of any negative physical attribute, including but not limited to water leaks, extreme floor or wall or ceiling cracks, insect infestation, appliance breakdown, or roof damage, the tenant will immediately notify landlord by phone or by written notice.

The tenant agrees to keep the property clean in and around the house and agrees to maintain proper sanitation of the area by preparing trash for pick-up by the regular trash service of the surrounding neighborhood, unless other arrangements have been made and agreed to in writing by the owner.

The tenant agrees to keep the lawn, landscaping, trees, and shrubberies neat, clean, mowed, trimmed, watered, and maintained as needed to ensure a healthy and visually appealing homestead, unless different arrangements have been agreed to in writing between landlord and tenant.

The tenant agrees to hold the landlord from any and all expense for lights, heat, water, or any other expense incident to the occupancy of said property, unless specifically agreed to in writing. The tenant agrees to keep these standard utilities connected and their corresponding bills paid

in a timely manner as required by the utility companies: _____

_____

Figure 2.   *(continued)*

(initials) _____

_____

If ANY utilities are not kept current, the tenant agrees to terminate this lease and give up the property's occupation at the landlord's discretion.

The tenant shall not engage in, or allow any other person, pet, or animal to engage in, any conduct that will disturb the quiet and peaceable enjoyment of the other tenants, neighbors, landlord, or use the property for any purpose whatsoever that violates the laws of the United States, the

State of _____, or the City of _____.

The tenant will keep no pets of any kind, inside or outside the property, without a separate and written consent of the landlord.

Time is the essence of this contract, and should the tenant default in the payment of any installment of the principal sum herein named, the total principal sum shall become immediately due and payable and the landlord shall be entitled to possession of the premises, at tenant's option

in accordance with the _____ Landlord and Tenant Act, and the landlord shall have the right to store and/or dispose of such property in accordance with said Act, and thereafter the tenant shall be liable to the landlord for any amounts uncollected from such disposition, and the expenses therefor, including a reasonable attorney's fee.

The property herein leased will be used for residential purposes only and for no other object or purpose and this lease shall not be sublet without the written consent of the landlord.

In the event of assignment to creditors by the tenant, or the institution of bankruptcy proceedings against the tenant, such events shall cancel and hold for naught this lease, and all the rights thereunder, and possession of said property shall immediately, by such act or acts, pass to the landlord at landlord's option.

The tenant shall pay a late fee of _____ in

addition to each monthly payment that is paid after the _____ day of any month within the terms of this lease. Starting on the

Figure 2.   *(continued)*

(initials) _____

_____

_____ day of the month, a late fee of _____
per day will be added to the existing late fee due.

The tenant will waive tenant's rights under the _____
Landlord and Tenant Act if the rent and all applicable late charges are not

paid in full by the _____ day of the month, immediately
relinquishing possession of the property to the landlord at the landlord's
request.

The tenant agrees to pay all rents and fees with a personal check,
money order, cashier's check, or cash. If a personal check is ever not
honored by the landlord's bank, for any reason whatsoever, the tenant
agrees to pay a check charge of *Ten Dollars ($10)* then pay with cash until
the expiration of this lease term.

The tenant shall check each and all smoke alarms weekly, replacing the
battery as needed with an alkaline battery to ensure that adequate warning is
provided. Also, the fire extinguisher's gauge will be checked monthly to make
sure the extinguisher's gauge indicates a full charge of pressure.

The tenant agrees to keep the window screens on the windows at all
times, paying a twenty-dollar ($20) service charge plus parts, if a screen is
removed or damaged in any way, for its replacement.

The tenant will let no more than _____ guest(s) stay
overnight for a maximum period of seven (7) consecutive days in any two-
month period without written consent from the landlord. This limitation

_____ apply to immediate children of the tenant.

The tenant _____ keep any water-filled furniture at the
property without the landlord's written consent.

The tenant agrees to keep no more than _____ vehicles,
including but not limited to trucks, motorcycles, and cars, on the
premises. These vehicles must be both operable and currently licensed.
The tenant agrees not to repair any vehicles on the premises if the repairs
will take more than 24 hours, without prior written consent from the
landlord. Tenant agrees not to keep off-road vehicles, including

Figure 2.   *(continued)*

but not limited to boats and trailers, without prior written consent from the landlord.

Landlord has obtained insurance to cover the landlord's interest and liability, but does *not* insure tenant's belongings or negligence.

The tenant will return any and all property-related keys upon lease termination, and give up Five Dollars ($5) per nonreturned key out of the security and cleaning deposit.

The tenant further agrees that after the expiration of the time given

in this lease, the _____ day of _____, without notice from the landlord, to give possession of property to landlord, and upon tenant's failure to do so shall become liable to the landlord for an additional one-month extension of this contract upon notice from the landlord.

Contact the landlord at _____

_____

(phone: _____).

IN WITNESS THEREOF, the parties hereto have hereunto set their hands the day and year first above written.

_____   _____

_____   _____
(Landlord or Agent)   (Tenant(s))

Figure 3.   *A month-to-month residence lease.*

Page 1 of 5

(initials) _____

_____

* Residence Month-to-Month Lease *

This month-to-month lease, made and entered into this _____ day of

_____, by and between _____, of

_____, _____, hereinafter called the "landlord," and

_____, of _____, _____,
hereinafter called the "tenant."

  The landlord owns the following described real estate and premises,

situated in _____ County, _____:

_____ .

  The landlord rents and leases to the tenant the above described

premises from the _____ day of _____, for each month
thereafter, until thirty (30) days' notice is properly served by either the
landlord or tenant, onto the other.

  The tenant promises and agrees to pay the landlord payments as

follows: _____ for the
security/cleaning deposit paid to landlord at the execution of this contract.
The entire security/cleaning deposit will be refunded to the tenant within
ten (10) days after tenant's normal lease termination or move-out,
whichever comes last, if the property is left in move-in condition and will
be escrowed in a safety bank account until such time. The security/
cleaning deposit's refundable amount will be prorated accordingly if the
property is left in less than acceptable condition. The sum of

_____ is already

paid for the first full month's rent of occupancy (_____). The sum

of _____ will be
payable on the first (1st) day of each and every month after this lease
signing, until notice is given by either the landlord or tenant to terminate
this lease, by serving thirty (30) days' notice to the other.

Figure 3.   *(continued)*

(initials) _____

_____

No part of said money shall be due and payable until the tenant has been placed in the actual possession of said premises with the keys needed to gain access. This has been done as of the date of this contract.

It is agreed that the tenant will keep and maintain all portions of the building let to him or her by the terms of this contract in as good a state of repair as the same are turned over to tenant. This means woodwork, walls, floors, ceilings, windows, screens, doors, carpet, shades, electric, grounds, plumbing, and outside storage, all of which may be inspected by the landlord on notice from the tenant of intent to vacate and in no event will this lease terminate unless the foregoing is acceptable to the landlord. Normal use without evident mars will not constitute violation.

The tenant agrees to be responsible to pay for the repair of any damage done to any of the buildings or grounds by any of tenant's family or guests. If the tenant notices any signs of property damage or signs of any negative physical attribute, including but not limited to water leaks, extreme floor or wall or ceiling cracks, insect infestation, appliance breakdown, or roof damage, the tenant will immediately notify landlord by phone or by written notice.

The tenant agrees to keep the property clean in and around the house and agrees to maintain proper sanitation of the area by preparing trash for pick-up by the regular trash service of the surrounding neighborhood, unless other arrangements have been made and agreed to in writing by the owner.

The tenant agrees to keep the lawn, landscaping, trees, and shrubberies neat, clean, mowed, trimmed, watered, and maintained as needed to ensure a healthy and visually appealing homestead, unless different arrangements have been agreed to in writing between landlord and tenant.

The tenant agrees to hold the landlord from any and all expense for lights, heat, water, or any other expense incident to the occupancy of said property, unless specifically agreed to in writing. The tenant agrees to keep these standard utilities connected and their corresponding bills paid

in a timely manner as required by the utility companies: _____

Figure 3.   *(continued)*

(initials) _____

_____

If ANY utilities are not kept current, the tenant agrees to terminate this lease and give up the property's occupation at the landlord's discretion.

The tenant shall not engage in, or allow any other person, pet, or animal to engage in, any conduct that will disturb the quiet and peaceable enjoyment of the other tenants, neighbors, landlord, or use the property for any purpose whatsoever that violates the laws of the United States, the

State of _____, or the City of _____.

The tenant will keep no pets of any kind, inside or outside the property, without a separate and written consent of the landlord.

Time is the essence of this contract, and should the tenant default in the payment of any installment sum herein named, the landlord shall be entitled to possession of the premises, at tenant's option in accordance

with the _____ Landlord and Tenant Act, and the landlord shall have the right to store and/or dispose of such property in accordance with said Act, and thereafter the tenant shall be liable to the landlord for any amounts uncollected from such disposition, and the expenses therefor, including a reasonable attorney's fee.

The property herein leased will be used for residential purposes only and for no other object or purpose and this lease shall not be sublet without the written consent of the landlord.

In the event of assignment to creditors by the tenant, or the institution of bankruptcy proceedings against the tenant, such events shall cancel and hold for naught this lease, and all the rights thereunder, and possession of said property shall immediately, by such act or acts, pass to the landlord at landlord's option.

The tenant shall pay a late fee of _____ in

addition to each monthly payment that is paid after the _____ day of any month within the terms of this lease. Starting on the

Figure 3.   *(continued)*

_____ day of the month, a late fee of _____ per day will be added to the existing late fee due.

The tenant will waive tenant's rights under the _____ Landlord and Tenant Act if the rent and all applicable late charges are not

paid in full by the _____ day of the month, immediately relinquishing possession of the property to the landlord at the landlord's request.

The tenant agrees to pay all rents and fees with a personal check, money order, cashier's check, or cash. If a personal check is ever not honored by the landlord's bank, for any reason whatsoever, the tenant agrees to pay a check charge of *Ten Dollars ($10)* then pay with cash until the expiration of this lease term.

The tenant shall check each and all smoke alarms weekly, replacing the battery as needed with an alkaline battery to ensure that adequate warning is provided. Also, the fire extinguisher's gauge will be checked monthly to make sure the extinguisher's gauge indicates a full charge of pressure.

The tenant agrees to keep the window screens on the windows at all times, paying a twenty-dollar ($20) service charge plus parts, if a screen is removed or damaged in any way, for its replacement.

The tenant will let no more than _____ guest(s) stay overnight for a maximum period of seven (7) consecutive days in any two-month period without written consent from the landlord. This limitation

_____ apply to immediate children of the tenant.

The tenant _____ keep any water-filled furniture at the property without the landlord's written consent.

The tenant agrees to keep no more than _____ vehicles, including but not limited to trucks, motorcycles, and cars, on the premises. These vehicles must be both operable and currently licensed. The tenant agrees not to repair any vehicles on the premises if the repairs will take more than 24 hours, without prior written consent from the landlord. Tenant agrees not to keep off-road vehicles, including

Figure 3.   *(continued)*

(initials) _____

_____

but not limited to boats and trailers, without prior written consent from the landlord.

Landlord has obtained insurance to cover the landlord's interest and liability, but does *not* insure tenant's belongings or negligence.

The tenant will return any and all property-related keys upon lease termination, and give up Five Dollars ($5) per nonreturned key out of the security and cleaning deposit.

The tenant agrees that after the expiration of the time given in this lease, by thirty (30) days' proper service by either the landlord or tenant to the other, to give possession of property to landlord, and upon tenant's failure to do so shall become liable to the landlord for an additional one-month extension of this contract upon notice from the landlord. This month-to-month lease remains in effect each month, until a proper thirty (30) days' notice is given by either the landlord or tenant to the other.

Contact the landlord at _____

_____

(phone: _____).

IN WITNESS THEREOF, the parties hereto have hereunto set their hands the day and year first above written.

_____   _____

_____   _____
(Landlord or Agent)   (Tenant(s))

Figure 4.   *A walk-through checklist.*

*** Please return with next rent payment ***

Walk-through Checklist

Dear Tenant:

Please take the time to go through each room to make sure everything works fine and is in good condition.

Outside of home:
_____Siding, shutters, windows, ground, screens, and storage building are in good shape and clean.

I feel I should bring the following to your attention:

_____

_____

Living room:
_____Carpet, walls, lights, outlets, ceilings, and miniblinds are in good shape and clean.

I feel I should bring the following to your attention:

_____

_____

Kitchen:
_____Shelves, sink, stove, floor, refrigerator, dishwasher, pipes, ceiling, and fan are all in good shape and clean.

I feel I should bring the following to your attention:

_____

_____

Bedrooms:
_____Carpet, walls, closets, miniblinds, ceilings, fans, and lights are all in good shape and clean.

I feel I should bring the following to your attention:

_____

_____

Figure 4.   *(continued)*

Bathrooms:
_____Floors, walls, toilets, sinks, tubs, and plumbing are all in good shape and clean.

I feel I should bring the following to your attention:

_____

_____

Other possible problems:

_____

_____

_____
Tenant's signature   Date

Figure 5.   *A sheet of information for new tenants.*

New Tenant Information

Landlord: Sam Garrett, 913 East Oak Road, Miami, FL 41156, 555-4321
Fire: 911 or 555-3234   **Police or Ambulance:** 911 or 555-2982
Post Office: 13 Sycamore Drive, 2 blocks north of home
Closest Shopping Center: 843 Oak Street, 1 block east

Please check the smoke/fire alarms WEEKLY. There is a button to press that will test them. One alarm is located in the upstairs hall close to the ceiling; the other is downstairs to the right of the bathroom. For your safety, please use a replacement 9-volt alkaline battery if yours fails. The batteries are easy to replace if you stand on a ladder or stepstool.

Please do NOT store any items in the air conditioner and heater closet. The air is to circulate throughout the closet and it is so important that you will be damaging the unit and will be responsible for ALL REPAIRS including replacement of the entire unit if needed. I trust you and I only put it this bluntly to show you how important it is to me that you understand.

If you see a leak, turn off the shutoff valve to the tub, toilet, or faucet. Call me as soon as you get the water turned off.

Obviously, if you see a water leak, shut it off if you can and call me. IF it is an emergency and it is about to cause major water damage because of its size, call a plumber. For most "average" problems, I would like to be called first. In an *extreme emergency*, call Donald's Plumbing at 555-1109.

* * * I have provided you with a plunger in the upstairs bathroom under the sink. It is VITAL that you help keep water off the floor in the upstairs bathroom, otherwise it will damage the ceiling and your furnishings downstairs if it comes through.

The electric breaker box to your home is located in the air conditioner and heater closet.

Please keep in mind that your lease extends to the outside storage building in back. Its floor, walls, and outside should be kept as clean and in as good condition as your house. If you leave oil drippings on the floor, I will have to keep part or all of the deposit. (Please use a pan if you store anything with an engine in there.)

Your fire extinguisher is under your kitchen sink. If you have to use it, pull the safety pin first. Check the gauge MONTHLY to make sure it

Figure 5. *(continued)*

---

is charged. If it is not charged, please let me know immediately. Usually, they hold their charge at least 2 years, so you should not have a problem often. *Please do NOT "test" it* by shooting it to try it out. This WILL discharge the unit and make it unusable.

Please treat this home with the care that it deserves. Please be aware of noise to your neighborhood. If your neighbors cause you trouble, please call me and I'll take care of it immediately. Conversely, they will call me if there is something you are doing that bothers them. I will let a house sit empty for several months rather than let someone move in who bothers the neighbors or who does damage to the rental property.

In return, I will be the nicest landlord you have EVER had, and if there is an emergency, I'll get it taken care of faster than you have ever seen. I care about you and want you to be as happy as possible.

Figure 6.   *A sample lease-change agreement.*

* Temporary Lease-Change Agreement *

From   until   ,   , "Landlord," and
, "Tenant" (both signed below), agree to modify temporarily, within the date limits just described, their lease agreement.

The Tenant agrees to pay the full monthly required rent in four weekly installments of   ($) due in the Landlord's possession on Friday of each week of the temporary time period.

There is no late statute or fee in this temporary lease amendment as no late payment will be accepted from the Tenant. If any installment is not paid on or before the due day of each week, the original lease agreement will take effect again, with the full past-due portion payable and due, and full eviction proceedings will begin.

Signed on   by:

_____   _____
(Landlord)   (Tenant)

Figure 7. *A sample eviction notice.*

---

* Notice of Eviction Proceedings *

, undersigned "Landlord," immediately requests the
vacancy of   , the "Tenant," currently in possession of the
property located at:

The Tenant is hereby requested to appear at the eviction and rent
collection hearing at   A.M.,   , at the
County Courthouse.

This eviction proceeding was initiated by the Landlord to collect all
past-due rents and fees and to require the immediate vacancy of the said
property by the Tenant. The past-due rent and fees sum to
              (\$).

This notice is signed on the following date by the Landlord:

_____   Date: _____
                            (Landlord)

On _____, _____
properly served this eviction notice.

Index